COMMUNICATION MODELS

COMMUNICATION MODELS

for the study of mass communications

second edition

DENIS McQUAIL
and
SVEN WINDAHL

PEARSON
Prentice
Hall

Harlow, England • London • New York • Boston • San Francisco • Toronto
Sydney • Tokyo • Singapore • Hong Kong • Seoul • Taipei • New Delhi
Cape Town • Madrid • Mexico City • Amsterdam • Munich • Paris • Milan

Pearson Education Limited
Edinburgh Gate
Harlow
Essex CM20 2JE
England

and Associated Companies throughout the world

Visit us on the World Wide Web at:
http://www.pearsoneduc.com

First published 1982
Second edition 1993

ISBN 0 582 03650 X PPR

British Library Cataloguing-in-Publication Data
A catalogue record for this book is available from the British Library.

Library of Congress Cataloging-in-Publication Data
McQuail, Denis.
    Communication models for the study of mass com-
munications / Denis McQuail, Sven Windahl. – 2nd
ed.
    p. cm.
    Includes bibliographical references and index.
    ISBN 0–582–03650–X
    1. Communication models. I. Windhal, Sven,
1942–. II. Title. P91.M375 1993
    302.23′0228–dc20   92-28665 CIP

12 11 10 9
07 06 05 04 03

Set by 13 in 10/12pt Univers

Produced by Pearson Education Asia Pte. Ltd.
Printed in Singapore (B&JO)

CONTENTS

1   INTRODUCTION

2   BASIC MODELS

1 INTRODUCTION

1.1 SCOPE AND PURPOSE

This book has a dual objective. On the one hand, it seeks to bring together and to present, in a succinct and accessible form, many of the models which have been developed to describe or explain the process of mass communication. On the other hand, it aims to represent the main lines of thought about mass communication which have emerged during 40 years of research. At certain points we have drawn our own models to reflect important conceptual developments or relatively new fields of enquiry. In this much revised edition, over ten years on, we have omitted some earlier models and added new ones, both in order to take account of developments in the field and to extend the range (especially in Chs 7 to 9). Some of the early basic models are certainly dated, but we have kept them for historical reasons and because they provided the foundations for later work.

There is more than one way of telling the history of ideas about mass communication and the one we have chosen follows a tradition in which mass communication can be seen as a specific form of a general phenomenon, in which the main elements of sender, message and receiver take on distinctive characteristics and meanings. We hope to shed light on these meanings by starting with some very simplified and general versions of what any communication relationship involves and then proceeding to deal with the effects of mass communication and with the relationships which hold amongst the main participants and between the participants and their society.

In focusing on mass communication, we have inevitably to neglect interesting developments in the study of inter- and intra-personal communication and of communication structures and flows within groups and organizations. Nevertheless, our own view of mass communication is of a process which is co-extensive and interactive with other types of communication network and process. While different specialisms have emerged in the study of communication which seem to have little in common by the way of theory, method or aim, we would prefer not to mark clear boundaries around the substance of any one 'communication system'. We anticipate a future in which existing boundaries will become even less clear than they are at present and when communication technology and new expressions of communication need will produce different structures, relationships and possibilities of effect.

1.2   THE USES AND MISUSES OF MODELS

In the first edition we commented on the relative lack of interest in communication models at that time. This no longer seems to be the case, presumably because the advantages we perceived are now more widely acknowledged. Even so, the potential advantages and drawbacks call for some further comment. For our purpose, we consider a model as a consciously simplified description in graphic form of a piece of reality. A model seeks to show the main elements of any structure or process and the relationships between these elements. Deutsch (1966) notes the following main advantages of models in the social sciences. Firstly, they have an *organizing function* by ordering and relating systems to each other and by providing us with images of wholes that we might not otherwise perceive. A model gives a *general* picture of a range of different particular circumstances. Secondly, it helps in *explaining*, by providing in a simplified way information which would otherwise be complicated or ambiguous. This gives the model a *heuristic function*, since it can guide the student or researcher to key points of a process or system. Thirdly, the model may make it possible to *predict* outcomes or the course of events. It can at least be a basis for assigning probabilities to various alternative outcomes, and hence for formulating hypotheses in research. Some models claim only to describe the structure of a phenomenon. In this sense, a diagram of the components of a radio set could be described as 'structural'. Other models, which we call 'functional', describe systems in terms of energy, forces and their direction, the relations between parts and the influence of one part on another.

The models presented in this book fall mainly into the latter category, simply because all communication is in some degree dynamic and involves some elements of process or change. Even so, some of the models are very simple and tell us little about the forces at work which relate elements to each other. While models in general can be purely verbal, or diagrammatic, or mathematical, we have presented only those which are both verbal and diagrammatic.

It has been argued against the use of models that they tend to trap their originators and users within rather limited confines which they then become eager to defend against attack. Such a tendency can have a delaying effect on the development of a science, although this has probably not happened in the case of communication research, where old models have tended to be soon discarded or modified. A similar risk is that a model, or even a succession of models, can tend to perpetuate some initial questionable, but fundamental, assumptions about the components of a model or the processes at work. An example in the field of communication is the tendency to represent communication as a one-directional process in which a 'sender' deliberately tries to influence a 'receiver'. Such a representation tends to deny the circularity, negotiability and openness of much communication.

It should at least be remembered that there are some risks in using models, even for heuristic purposes. They are inevitably incomplete, oversimplified and involve some concealed assumptions. There is certainly no model that is suitable for all purposes and all levels of analysis and it is important to choose the correct model for the purpose one has in mind. One of the purposes of the book is to give some indication of the proper purpose and level of different models, partly by showing how they have been used in communication research. The reader should become aware of the possibilities of testing models against circumstances or cases and of adapting any given model to suit the chosen application. The models presented are not so sacred that they cannot easily be given a somewhat different shape and formulation. It should become apparent that anyone is in a position to

construct their own models of a given aspect of the communication process and we hope that this book will encourage students of mass communication to adopt this process as a means
of elucidation.

We view models primarily as aids to thought which are especially appropriate in the study of communication. Why they
should be so appropriate is not easy to demonstrate, but it may
stem from the fact that communication is a binding force in social
relationships without at the same time being visible or having
tangible and permanent forms. Acts of communication take predictable or recurrent forms within a given structure of relationships and have consequences for this structure without being
readily open to observation. There is, consequently, an attraction
in being able to 'draw' the 'lines' which stand for the links we
know to exist but cannot see and to use other devices to show the
structure, topography, strength and direction of relationships. So
much of the subject of communication has to be dealt with in
verbal abstractions that it is an aid and a relief to have at least
something 'fixed' in graphic form, however much the element of
abstraction may remain.

1.3   DEFINITIONS AND TERMS

The central concept in this book is communication. It has been
defined in a number of ways, but we do not wish or need to be
tied to one particular definition, since the authors we refer to have
different notions of the concept. But the following examples give
us some idea of the variety of meanings involved:

> The transmission of information, ideas, attitudes, or emotion from one
> person or group to another (or others) primarily through symbols (Theo-
> dorson and Theodorson 1969)
>
> In the most general sense, we have communication wherever one
> system, a source, influences another, the destination, by manipulation
> of alternative symbols, which can be transmitted over the channel con-
> necting them (Osgood *et al.* 1957)
>
> Communication may be defined as 'social interaction through mess-
> ages' (Gerbner 1967)

Thus, in the most general terms, communication implies a sender, a channel, a message, a receiver, a relationship between sender and receiver, an effect, a context in which communication occurs and a range of things to which 'messages' refer. Sometimes, but not always, there is an intention, or purpose to 'communicate' or to 'receive'. Communication can be any or all of the following: an *action on* others; an *interaction with* others and a *reaction to* others.

Sometimes the originators of models point to two additional processes, that of 'encoding' (at the sender end of the model) and that of 'decoding' (at the receiver end). Encoding means that the message is translated into a language or code suitable for the means of transmission and the intended receivers. Decoding refers to the re-translation of the message in order to extract meaning. In a conversation between two persons, the encoding function is performed by the speech mechanism and (for non-verbal communication) muscles making possible gestures, etc. In such a case, the senses of hearing and sight perform the decoding function. In mass communication encoding can refer to technical transformations necessary for the transmission of signals and also to the systematic choice of words, pictures and formats according to established procedures and the expectations held about audience experience.

In many models, the concept of 'feedback' is employed. In general, this refers to any process by which the communicator obtains information about whether and how the intended receiver has indeed received the message. Such information can help to modify ongoing or future communication behaviour. In a face-to-face communication situation this may take the form of questions, requests to repeat something, gestures, responses and so on. In mass communication, feedback of these kinds is mainly replaced by: audience research; sales figures; studio audiences; tryouts; letters and phone calls. But it can also take the form of response directly from superiors, colleagues, friends and other personal contacts.

As we have seen, many of the basic terms in communication take different meanings when they refer to mass communication and we need to have a different characterization of the latter. A **frequently cited definition is as follows:**

> Mass communications comprise the institutions and techniques by which specialized groups employ technological devices (press, radio, films, etc.) to disseminate symbolic content to large, heterogeneous and widely dispersed audiences (Janowitz 1968)

This points to most of the variations and additions that we need to take account of. The 'sender' in mass communication is always part of an organized group and often a member of an institution which has functions other than communication. The 'receiver' is always an individual but may often be seen by the sending organization as a group or collectivity with certain general attributes. The channel no longer consists of the social relationship, means of expression and sensory organs, but includes large-scale technologically based distribution devices and systems. These systems still have a social component, since they depend on law, custom and expectation. The message in mass communication is not a unique and transitory phenomenon, but a mass-produced and infinitely repeatable symbolic structure, often of great complexity.

Of particular significance in mass communication are: the public and open nature of all communication; the limited and controlled access to 'sending' facilities; the impersonality of the relationship between sender and receiver; the imbalance of the relationship between them; the intervention of institutionalized arrangements between sender and receiver. In reality, there is no single universal form of the mass communication process and the diversity of the reality accounts in part for the multiplicity of possible models to represent the whole or parts of it.

1.4   EARLY COMMUNICATION MODELS AND MASS COMMUNICATION RESEARCH

Mass communication research, stimulated primarily by concern over the political influence of the mass press and later over the moral and social consequences of film and radio, extends back at least until the beginning of the present century. Research into communication in general had its origins in the wish to test and increase efficiency and effectiveness in the spheres of education, propaganda, telecommunication, advertising and public and human relations. Research activity began with practical concerns and was fed by developments in psychology and sociology and by general advances in methodology, especially the use of experiments, social surveys and statistics.

It was not really until after the Second World War that a focus on communication as such was articulated. Just as much early empirical research was largely an American phenomenon, so it was in the United States in the post-war period that the possibility of a science of communication was first discussed. The decade of the 1950s proved to be fertile in model-building activity, which can be taken as an expression of the search for growth and unity in the study of communication. According to Johnson and Klare (1961), it was a mathematician, Claude Shannon, who first provided the stimulus to social scientists to formulate their thinking about communication in model form according to the terms outlined above. The initial appeal of this approach can probably be related, first of all, to the predominance of the current interest in effects and effectiveness, secondly to its consistency with the stimulus–response model of behaviour control and learning which was fundamental to psychology (see 3.1) and thirdly, to the growing wish to order and codify existing knowledge and enquiry in mass-communication research.

1.5 ELABORATION OF THE BASIC MATHEMATICAL MODEL

The simple sender–channel–message–receiver model was rapidly modified during the 1950s according to the interests both of the students of interpersonal communication and of mass communication. The changes took account of several important aspects of human communication. One was the need to incorporate more fully and as an essential component, the occurrence of feedback. Associated with this is the recognition of the non-linearity of communication processes. They are typically circular, recurrent and spiralling, since the change brought about by communication initiates a new 'loop' at a different point and on a different plane (to use spatial analogies) than at the start. These are discussed in 2.2, in connection with the work of Osgood, Schramm and Dance.

A second major development is related to the fact that receivers normally selectively perceive, interpret and retain messages. The potential inefficiency of a communication link was, of course, recognized in the earlier mathematical model, but the problem is there treated as 'noise' in the system, since the main criteria of successful communication are derived from the intentions of the sender. Gerbner's model (2.3) incorporates a solution to the problem which recognizes the substantive interest of the sources and nature of apparent inefficiency. He stresses the essentially *transactional* character of much communication and the dependence of any meaning which is acquired on the assumptions and foreknowledge of the receiver and on the context in which communication takes place. One might sum up this development as having to do with the intersubjectivity of communication, since all communication involves more or less elaborate exchange and bargaining between senders and receivers. The result of communication is thus a matter of negotiation and cannot always be predicted in advance. This thought has continued to be important in recent work on interpersonal communication and has influenced the development of what we have labelled 'audience-centred' approaches to mass communication (Ch. 5).

1.6 FROM COMMUNICATION TO MASS COMMUNICATION

An early point of departure in the model-making tradition was the separation out of models concerned expressly with mass communication. It was essential to make specific allowance for the distinctive features of mass communication which have been briefly described. The work of Westley and Maclean (2.5) was especially important in emphasizing the role of the media organization in controlling the channels of mass communication and in mediating relations between sources in society and the general public. Their model also bridges the gap between the original basic model of communication, with its emphasis on purposive transmission of messages, and the seemingly purposeless flow of mass communication. In their model, the mass communicator acts as an agent for the receiver, an interpreter of needs and interests. The process is guided more by anticipated audience demand than by communicator purpose. Maletzke's model (2.6) develops some of these ideas and also firmly reminds us that both mass communicator and audience operate within a social context and a small group environment. The chapter on basic models ends with a reminder that communication (including mass communication) is not only or always a linear process of transmission but can have important 'ritual', expressive and participant aspects and can also be guided by other logics, for instance that of gaining and keeping the attention of spectators (see 2.6 and 2.7).

1.7 DEVELOPMENTS IN COMMUNICATION MODELS AND COMMUNICATION RESEARCH

During the 1960s and 1970s, the focus of research interest tended to shift away from questions of direct effects of mass media on opinions, attitudes and behaviour, although these topics are still covered below, especially in Chapter 3. More attention was paid to longer-term and indirect socializing and ideological processes (see 4.2 and 4.4) and also to effects which depend on the relative degree of attention paid by the media to aspects of the social environment (see 4.3 and 4.5). The influence of mass society theory, which conceived the citizens of modern societies to be vulnerable to media manipulation on the part of power-wielding élites, gave way to theory in which people themselves played a more active role in adopting or rejecting the guidelines offered by the mass media. The media are more likely to offer the 'raw material', as it were, for forming opinions and constructing a view of the world, than to impose their definitions. Such ideas have been reinforced by theories of an active audience (Ch. 5) and by theories concerning the differential reception of media texts which have empowered the audience as 'decoder' and reader (5.3).

Despite these tendencies to play down the one-directional power of the media, the strong growth of critical theory during the 1970s and 1980s kept alive the perception that mass media are not simply neutral channels of social influence, but are more likely to increase the advantage of those with most economic and political power. They do not, for instance, seem to work to diminish structural inequalities in information (4.5). A healthy suspicion of continued media influence in society has led to much attention to the media organization and its relation to pressures and constraints in its environment (Ch. 6), especially those which can affect news selection and presentation.

This revised edition has been expanded to take account of three fields of research and theory which have been growing in salience. One is far from new, but deserves separate attention, and relates to 'applied communication' – the purposeful use of mass media for influencing attitudes or behaviour or for large-scale informational campaigns (Ch. 7). The other two wholly new sections take up topics which were anticipated in the Introduction to the first edition, ten years ago. These deal, respectively, with aspects of the emerging 'Information Society' and with international communication. We are moving into an era when the boundary separating mass communication from other communication processes is becoming much less clear. The 'ideal type' of a centralized broadcasting or publishing organization sending out the same content to large and stable audiences is less and less appropriate. The clear distinction and fixed relation between a collective 'sender' and a collective 'receiver' no longer holds good, both for reasons of changing technology and because of the growth of new forms of media policy and organization. The mass-communication process continues to diversify and fragment. Observers have noted a process of convergence of modes of communication technology and a breakdown of traditional lines of distinction between media (Pool 1983) (see 8.3).

The accelerating 'internationalization' of mass communication flow has been both hailed as a benefit and also problematized for the potential social and cultural harm that it may cause. The issues which are raised by the models discussed in Chapter 9 are not especially new, but they remain urgent. One of the directions for model-building which we anticipated in our earlier edition concerned differences between types of national media system, especially because of ideological differences. The decline of communist systems in Europe and the resurgence of free-market forms of organization, coupled with the technological change and convergence noted above have made this a less relevant concern, although important differences do remain between social systems in the perception of communication problems and in the ways in which these may be tackled (8.4).

1.8   FUTURE DEVELOPMENTS

We feel less able to predict the course of future model-building than we did ten years ago, mainly because so much is changing. Perhaps the most significant developments in the coming decade will follow from the changing balance of communication flows, as outlined in section 8.2., and from the increasing interrelation between different kinds of communication. We are even more inclined than before to rule out the likelihood or desirability of any single comprehensive communication model. As before, we would like to stress the utility of model-making as a continuing activity designed to clarify new ideas and theories and helping to organize research findings and point to questions for research. Models will have to be adapted to the changing communication reality of our societies.

References   Deutsch, K. (1966) *The Nerves of Government*. New York: Free Press.

Gerbner, G. (1967) 'Mass media and human communication theory' in Dance, F.E.X. (ed.), *Human Communication Theory*. New York: Holt, Rinehart and Winston.

Janowitz, M. (1968) 'The study of mass communication' in Sills, D.E. (ed.), *International Encyclopedia of the Social Sciences*. New York: Macmillan and Free Press, vol. 3, p. 41.

Johnson, F.C. and **Klare, G.R.** (1961) 'General models of communication research: a survey of a decade', *Journal of Communication*, **11**: 13–26.

Osgood, C.E., Suci, G.J. and **Tannenbaum, P.H.** (1957) *The Measurement of Meaning*. Urbana: University of Illinois Press.

Pool, I. de Sola (1983) *Technologies of Freedom*. Harvard, MA: Belknap Press.

Theodorson, S.A. and **Theodorson, A.G.** (1969) *A Modern Dictionary of Sociology*. New York: Cassell.

2   BASIC MODELS

2.1   THE LASSWELL FORMULA

The American political scientist Harold D. Lasswell began an article in 1948 with perhaps the most famous single phrase in communication research: 'A convenient way to describe an act of communication is to answer the following questions:

Who?
Says what?
In which channel?
To whom?
With what effect?'

This has ever since been known and cited as the Lasswell Formula, and if transformed to a graphic model it gives the diagram as in Fig. 2.1.1.

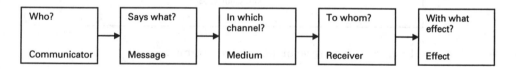

Fig. 2.1.1   The Lasswell Formula with corresponding elements of the communication process (Lasswell 1948).

This simple formula has been used in several ways, mostly to organize and to give structure to discussions about communication (cf. Riley and Riley 1959). Lasswell himself uses it to point out distinct types of communication research. To each question he has attached a particular type of analysis **as is visualized in Fig. 2.1.2.**

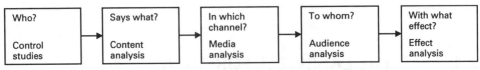

Fig. 2.1.2   The Lasswell Formula with corresponding fields of communication research.

Having found the Lasswellian model useful although some-what too simple, some researchers have developed it further. Braddock (1958) found that there are more considerations to work with than those five presented by Lasswell.

In his version of the model, Braddock adds two more facets of the communicative act, namely the circumstances under which a message is sent, and for what purpose the communicator says something. We may represent this as in Fig. 2.1.3.

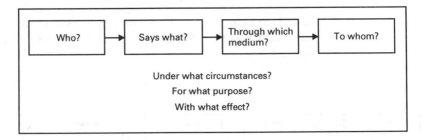

Fig. 2.1.3   Braddock's extension of the Lasswell Formula.

Comment   The Lasswell Formula shows a typical trait of early communi-cation models: it more or less takes for granted that the commu-nicator has some intention of influencing the receiver and, hence, that communication should be treated mainly as a persuasive process. It is also assumed that messages always have effects. Models such as this have surely contributed to the tendency to exaggerate the effects of, especially, mass communication. On the other hand, this is not surprising when we know that Lass-well's interest at the time was political communication and propaganda. For analysing political propaganda, the formula is well suited.

Braddock stresses that the formula may be misleading in that it directs the researcher to distinct fields of study. In reality they are to a large extent interrelated.

Lasswell has been further criticized for having omitted the element of feedback. In this way, too, his model reflects the general view of the time when it was formulated. This criticism, however, should not obscure the fact that it is even today a convenient and comprehensive way of introducing people to the study of the communication process.

References   **Braddock, R.** (1958) 'An extension of the "Lasswell Formula", *Journal of Communication*, **8**: 88–93.

Lasswell, H.D. (1948) 'The structure and function of communication in society' in Bryson, (ed.), *The Communication of Ideas.* New York: Harper and Brothers.

Riley, J.W. and **Riley, M.W.** (1959) 'Mass communication and the social system' in Merton, R.K., Broom, L. and Cottrell, S. (eds), *Sociology Today.* New York: Basic Books.

2.2   SHANNON AND WEAVER'S, OSGOOD AND SCHRAMM'S, AND DANCE'S MODELS

In spite of the many differences between them, the first two models to be described have in common that they have both been very influential in the short history of mass communication research. The first of them was developed by the mathematician Claude Shannon in the late 1940s. The second is based on the ideas of the psycholinguist C.E. Osgood and was further developed and presented by the mass communication researcher Wilbur Schramm in the early 1950s. A third and more recent model, the helical, proposed by F.E.X. Dance, ends the chapter.

Shannon and Weaver

Johnson and Klare (1961) say in their review of communication models:

> Of all single contributions to the widespread interest in models today, Shannon's is the most important. For the technical side of communication research, Shannon's mathematical formulations were the stimulus to much of the later effort in this area.

We will not discuss here the mathematical aspects of Shannon's work. Let us just note that he worked for the Bell Telephone Laboratory and that his theories and models primarily applied to its particular field of communication, involving questions such as: Which kind of communication channel can bring through the maximum amount of signals? How much of a transmitted signal will be destroyed by noise while travelling from transmitter to receiver?

These are questions mostly dealt with within the field of information theory. Nevertheless the graphical model, made by Shannon and his co-worker Warren Weaver (1949), has been used analogically by behavioural and linguistic scientists. Technological problems differ of course from human ones, but it is easy to find the traces of the Shannon–Weaver model in a number of later models of human communication.

Communication is here described as a linear, one-way process. The model states five functions to be performed and notes one dysfunctional factor, noise. Graphically, it may be presented as in Fig. 2.2.1.

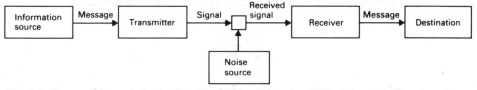

Fig. 2.2.1   Shannon and Weaver's 'mathematical model' describes communication as a linear, one-way process (Shannon and Weaver 1949).

First in the process is the *information source*, producing a *message* or a *chain of messages* to be communicated. In the next step, the message is formed into *signals* by a *transmitter*. The signals should be adapted to the *channel* leading to the *receiver*. The function of the receiver is the opposite of that of the transmitter. The receiver reconstructs the message from the signal. The *received message* then reaches the *destination*. The signal is vulnerable in so far as it may be disturbed by *noise*, interference which may occur, for example, when there are many signals in the same channel at the same time. This may result in a difference between transmitted and received signal, which, in its turn, may mean that the message produced by the source and that reconstructed by the receiver and having reached the destination do not have the same meaning. The inability on the part of communicators to realize that a sent and a received message are not always identical, is a common reason why communication fails.

DeFleur's development

DeFleur (1970) developed the Shannon and Weaver model further in a discussion about the correspondence between the meaning of the produced and the received message. He notes that in the communication process, 'meaning' is transformed into 'message' and describes how the transmitter transforms 'message' into 'information', which then passes through a channel (for example a mass medium). The receiver decodes the 'information' as a 'message', which in its turn is transformed at the destination into 'meaning'. If there is a correspondence between the two 'meanings' the result is communication. But, as DeFleur says, this correspondence is seldom perfect.

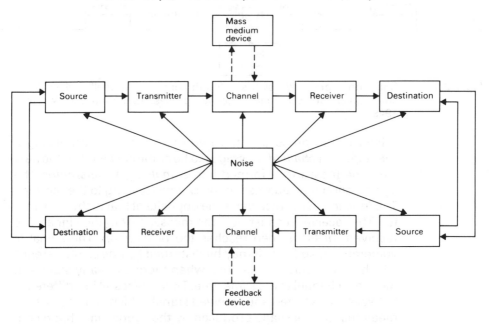

Fig. 2.2.2   DeFleur's development of the Shannon and Weaver model, allowing for feedback (DeFleur 1970).

In Fig. 2.2.2, DeFleur adds another set of components to the original Shannon and Weaver model to show how the source gets its feedback, which gives the source a possibility of adapting more effectively its way of communicating to the destination. This increases the possibility of achieving correspondence between the meanings (isomorphism). Shannon and Weaver's model is thus supplemented in an important way. Their model has been criticized for its linearity and lack of feedback. These features are accounted for in DeFleur's version, although it may be noted that in the case of mass communication, the sources (communicators) get only limited or indirect feedback from the audience. We return to this problem again elsewhere in the book (e.g., 2.5, 2.7, 6.3).

The Osgood and Schramm circular model

The next model of this chapter was presented by Wilbur Schramm (1954) and originated with C.E. Osgood. If the Shannon model could be described as linear, we may say that the Osgood–Schramm model is highly circular. Another difference lies in that whereas Shannon's interest is primarily directed to the *channels* mediating between the senders and receivers, Schramm and Osgood devote their discussion to the behaviour of the main *actors* in the communication process. Even so, there are important similarities between the two approaches.

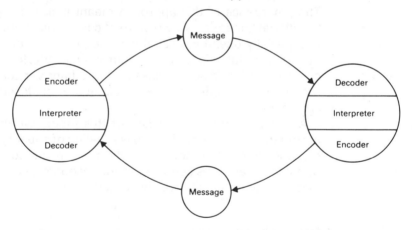

Fig. 2.2.3   In Osgood and Schramm's model both parties in, for example, a conversation fulfil the same functions (Schramm 1954).

Shannon and Weaver make a distinction between source and transmitter and between receiver and destination. In other words, two functions are fulfilled at the transmitting end of the process and two at the receiving end. In the Schramm–Osgood case, almost the same functions are performed, even if they do not talk about transmitters and receivers (see Fig. 2.2.3). They describe the acting parties as equals, performing identical functions, namely *encoding, decoding* and *interpreting*. Roughly, the encoding function is similar to the transmitting, the decoding to the receiving. Schramm and Osgood's interpreting function is fulfilled in Shannon and Weaver's model by the source and the destination. (For a discussion of the terms of the model, see 1.3.)

Comment   The traditional linear communication model clearly fixes and separates the roles of sender and receiver and it has from time to time been criticized for doing so. In a comment, Schramm (1954) remarks that

> In fact, it is misleading to think of the communication process as starting somewhere and ending somewhere. It is really endless. We are little switchboard centers handling and rerouting the great endless current of information . . .

The emergence of this approach meant a clear break with the traditional linear/one-way picture of communication. The model is especially useful in describing interpersonal communication but is less suitable for cases without, or with little, feedback. Mass communication is such a case and in a later version Schramm modified this model to make it adequate for describing mass communication.

A possible point of criticism of this model would lie in the argument that the model conveys a feeling of equality in communication. Very often communication is, on the contrary, fairly unbalanced as far as communication resources, power and time given to communicate are concerned.

Dance's helical model

Dance's helical model of communication is more recent, compared to the two models earlier presented in this chapter, and it is presented here solely because it may be seen as an interesting development of the Osgood and Schramm circular model.

In a discussion about linear versus circular communication models, Dance (1967) notes that today most people would regard the circular approach as that most adequate for describing the communication process. But it has its shortcomings as well. It

suggests that communication comes back, full circle, to exactly the same point from which it started. This part of the circular analogy is manifestly erroneous . . .

The helix provides understanding in some cases where the circle fails. It directs one's attention to the fact that the communication process moves forward and that what is communicated now will influence the structure and content of communication coming later on.

Most models in this volume give a sort of 'frozen' picture of the communication process. Dance underlines the *dynamic* nature of communication (see Fig. 2.2.4). The communication process, like all social processes, contains elements, relations and environments that are continually changing. The helix describes how different aspects of the process change over time. In a conversation, for example, the cognitive field is constantly widening for the parties or actors involved. The actors continually get more and more information about the actual topic, about the other's point of view, knowledge, etc.

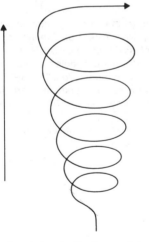

Fig. 2.2.4   Dance's helical model, showing the dynamic nature of the communication process (Dance 1967).

The helix takes on different shapes in different situations and for different individuals. For some, the helix tends to widen very much, because of prior knowledge of the topic, whereas for others with little basic knowledge, the helix expands moderately. The model may be used to illustrate information gaps (see 4.5) and the thesis that knowledge tends to create more knowledge. It may also illustrate communication situations such as the one where a lecturer in a series of lectures on the same subject assumes that the audience becomes successively better informed, which enables him/her in every new lecture to take this for granted and to structure the presentation accordingly.

Comment   Dance's model is, of course, not a tool for detailed analysis. Its worth lies in that it reminds us of the dynamic nature of communication, something that is otherwise too easily forgotten.

It would not go too far to say that the concept of the 'communicating man' here is more positive than in most other models. One gets the notion from this model that man, when communicating, is active, creative and able to store information, whereas many other models depict the individual rather as a passive creature.

References   Dance, F.E.X. (1967) 'A helical model of communication' in Dance, F.E.X. (ed.), *Human Communication Theory*. New York: Holt, Rinehart and Winston.
Defleur, M.L. (1966) *Theories of Mass Communication*. New York: David McKay.
Johnson, F.C. and Klare, G.R. (1961) 'General models of communication research: a survey of a decade', *Journal of Communication*, **11**: 13–26.
Schramm, W. (1954) 'How communication works' in Schramm, W. (ed.), *The Process and Effects of Mass Communication*. Urbana: University of Illinois Press.
Shannon, C. and Weaver, W. (1949) *The Mathematical Theory of Communication*. Urbana: University of Illinois Press.

2.3 GERBNER'S GENERAL MODEL OF COMMUNICATION

As the title indicates, the aim of the American mass-media researcher George Gerbner has been to sketch a model with a wide range of applications. It was first presented in 1956.

A special feature of this model is that it may be given different shapes depending on what kind of communication situation it describes. Its parts can be used as building blocks, which make it possible to describe simple as well as complicated communication processes as one of production (of messages) and of perception (of messages and of events to communicate about). The model allows us to put forward questions about the nature of and interplay between perception and production.

The model is given a verbal as well as a graphic version, and although we will concentrate on the latter, here is Gerbner's almost Lasswellian (see p. 13) formula:

1. Someone
2. perceives an event
3. and reacts
4. in a situation
5. through some means
6. to make available materials
7. in some form
8. and context
9. conveying content
10. with some consequence

Not all of these stages and elements appear in the basic graphic model (Figs 2.3.1 and 2.3.2), which, anyhow, may be said to start with an act of perception. What is perceived (Fig. 2.3.1) is marked E (event) and the perceiver, M, perceives the event as E^1. When the model refers to human communication, M may be a person, in a non-human context M may be a machine of some sort (e.g. a thermostat in a heating system).

The relation between E, M and E^1 is one of perception, and as students of mass communications we may use different approaches to this relation. Gerbner discusses a dimension of

approaches with two extremes. One extreme is the 'transactional' in which E^1 primarily is regarded as a function of M's
'assumptions, point of view, experiential background and other
related factors'. What E^1 will look like to M depends, thus, on
factors within or tied to M. The other extreme Gerbner labels
'psychophysical'. There E in itself is the most important factor,
giving rise to a perception of 'fidelity and adequacy under favourable conditions'.

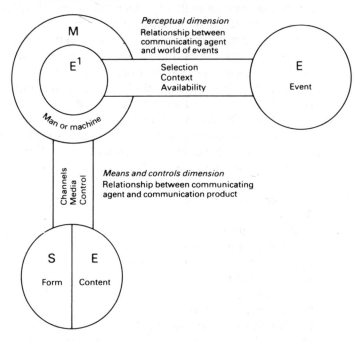

Fig. 2.3.1   Gerbner's general model of communication: M perceives E as E^1
(Gerbner 1956).

What will be perceived by M is determined by his/her way of
selecting, the context in which the E in question is to be found and
the degree of availability of this and other E's.

In the next step of the model it is assumed that M wants to
communicate about E^1 to someone else. M produces message SE
(statement about event). S here stands for 'shape, form', while E
is 'content'. Gerbner notes that 'S never stands by itself, unless it

signifies noise; it is always coupled with E, the representational, content qualities of the signal . . .'

To send the SE, M is dependent upon channels – media over which he has control to a higher or a lower degree.

The message (SE) may in its turn be perceived by another communication agent (M^2). In the same way as E was perceived by M as E^1, SE will be perceived by M^2 as SE^1. What was said earlier about different ways of approaching perception is valid for the relation $SE-M^2-SE^1$ as well. We can now see how the model is built up as a perception–production–perception chain, exemplified by Gerbner as in Fig. 2.3.2. The event, condensation of moisture in the air, is perceived by M as 'rain', which gives rise to the statement about the event, 'it's raining', which in turn is perceived or understood by M^2 as 'it's raining'. This model suggests that the human communication process may be regarded as subjective, selective, variable and unpredictable and that human communication systems are open systems.

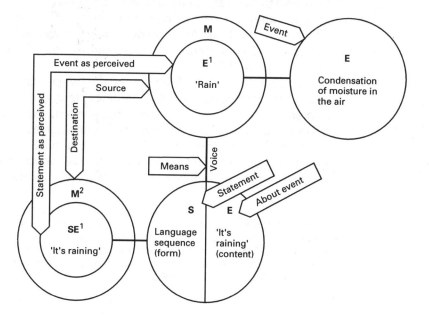

Fig. 2.3.2   Gerbner's model exemplified: M communications to M^2 a perception of the weather (Gerbner 1956).

The two different approaches to perception discussed above may easily be exemplified in mass communication research, in which given stimuli were expected to produce a predictable quantity of response, whereas one can notice that today's research more readily accepts the 'transactional' way of looking at perception.

Comment   In his original article, Gerbner demonstrates how his model can be used for several purposes. It may, for example, be built to describe mixed human and mechanical communication. It is also used to distinguish between different areas of research and theory building, just as Lasswell used his formula. Gerbner (1964) drew on his own model to illustrate and explain the main procedures of content analysis.

The flexible character of this model makes it useful on different levels. On the individual-to-individual level it may, for example, be useful to illustrate communicative and perceptual problems in the psychology of witnessing before a court: How adequate is the perception of witness M of event E, and how well is E^1 expressed in SE, and to what degree does the perception SE^1 of judge M^2 correspond to SE?

On a societal level, let E be potential news or just reality, let M stand for mass media, SE for media content and M^2 for media audience. We then have a model that gives us the possibility of asking questions such as 'How good is the correspondence between reality and the stories (between E and SE) about reality given by the media (M)' and 'How well is media content (SE) understood by the media audience (M^2)?' (cf. Gerbner 1964).

References   **Gerbner, G**. (1956) 'Toward a general model of communication', *Audio-Visual Communication Review*, **4**: 171–99.

Gerbner, G. (1964) 'On content analysis and critical research in mass communication' in Dexter, L.A. and White, D.M. (eds), *People, Society and Mass Communications*. New York: The Free Press.

2.4 NEWCOMB'S ABX MODEL, OTHER 'BALANCE' MODELS AND CO-ORIENTATION

2.4.1 The Newcomb ABX model

The main model to be discussed in this section is a very simple representation of the dynamics of communicative relationships between two individuals, but it lies at the heart of a wide-ranging body of ideas about attitude change, public opinion formation and propaganda.

The model shown in Fig. 2.4.1 was formulated by Newcomb (1953) and is an extension of earlier work by the psychologist Heider (1946). Heider had been concerned with the degree of consistency or inconsistency which might exist between two persons in relation to a third person or object. His theory held that in the case of two people who have an attitude of like or dislike towards each other and towards an external object, some patterns of relationship will be balanced (as when two persons like each other and also both like the object) and some will be unbalanced (as when two persons like each other, but one likes the object and the other does not, etc). Further, where there is balance, each participant will resist change and where there is imbalance, attempts will be made to restore 'cognitive' balance.

Heider was mainly concerned with cognitive processes *internal* to either of the two participants and Newcomb's development was to apply the theory to communication *between* two or more people. He postulated a 'strain to symmetry' as a result of which the area of agreement would be widened by engaging in communication. He made the assumption that 'communication performs the essential function of enabling two or more individuals to maintain simultaneous orientations to each other and towards objects of an external environment'. Communication is thus a 'learned response to strain' and we are likely to find 'more'

communication activity (information giving, seeking and exchange) under conditions of uncertainty and disequilibrium.

The model takes the form of a triangle, the points of which
represent, respectively, two individuals A and B and an object X
in their common environment. Both individuals are orientated to
one another and to X and communication is conceived of as the
process which supports the orientation structure, in the sense of
maintaining or improving the symmetry of the relationship between the three elements by transmitting information about any
change and by allowing adjustments to occur. The basic assumption of the model is that strain towards consistency of attitude
and relationship will instigate communication, where conditions
permit.

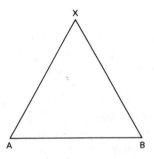

Fig. 2.4.1   Newcomb's model, in which two individuals (A and B) are orientated
towards each other and to an object (X) (Newcomb 1953).

The main propositions which can be derived from the model
are: that discrepancies between A and B in their orientation
towards X will stimulate communication: and that the effect of
this communication will tend to restore balance, which is postulated as the 'normal state' of a system of relationships.

Subsequently, Newcomb (1959) added some qualifications to
his earlier proposition by noting that communication is only
likely to be activated under certain conditions: (a) where there is
strong attraction between persons; (b) where the object is important to at least one of the participants; and (c) where the object X

has a joint relevance for both. Newcomb tested and evaluated this theory by research on the development over time of consensus amongst students who began as strangers and spent time together in the same student accommodation.

Work along similar lines was being carried out at approximately the same time by the social psychologist Festinger (1957), whose theory of cognitive dissonance held that decisions, choices and new information have a potential for creating a feeling of inconsistency for an individual, that such dissonance is 'psychologically uncomfortable' and will motivate the individual concerned to seek information which supports the choice which has been made. An example of the theory in operation is provided by evidence which showed that new car owners read advertisements about the car which they had recently bought more than they read advertisements about other cars.

Comment   In general, the kind of process indicated by the Newcomb model and predicted by balance theory as a whole supports the view that people are likely to attend to sources of information which are in line with their existing positions and look for information which supports and confirms their actual behaviour. It gives weight to theories of selective perception and to the expectation that the most likely effects of communication, including mass communication, will be towards the reinforcement of existing opinions, attitudes and behavioural tendencies. There is independent evidence from studies of the effects of mass communication (e.g. in Klapper 1960) which leads to the same conclusion.

We should, nevertheless, be careful not to assume that the tendency to consensus is the only cause and effect of communication. There is more than one way of resolving the 'uncertainty' or 'discomfort' which goes with cognitive discrepancy, for instance by forming new relationships or by finding further confirmation of divergence of view.

It is also important to remember that we cannot directly apply generalizations relating to processes internal to individuals or pertaining to small groups directly to large-scale situations, especially those at the level of a society. Societies do not have the same 'need' for consensus as single personalities or small groups and may be said to 'need' conflict and diversity in the interest of development.

2.4.2   Kite co-orientation model

More recently, a school of research in communication has flourished which has developed out of the ideas of balance, congruence and seeking of supportive information, which have already been discussed. The label 'co-orientation approach' has been given (by McLeod and Chaffee 1973) to this new tradition, which has its origins both in the work of Newcomb and also in early sociological concerns relating to symbolic interactionism. The key features of the approach are as follows: a focus on interpersonal communication or communication between groups – i.e., on communication which is two-way and interactive; an emphasis on the simultaneous inclusion in any study of the three main elements of information sources, communicators and

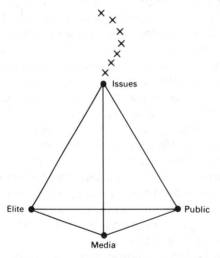

Fig. 2.4.2   A 'kite' co-orientation model, showing the relations between élite, media, public and issues.

receivers; an interest in the dynamics of communication situations. The basic features of the approach are illustrated in Fig.

2.4.2 in the form of a kite, which shows the relationship between the elements mentioned in a social setting. (The kite model was first presented on ice at Harlov Lake, Sweden, March 1980.)

The elements shown are largely self-explanatory. 'Elite' normally refers to a one-sided political interest. 'Issues' are any matter of current public debate, about which there will be items of information (shown as a set of Xs). The public is the relevant community affected and also the audience for the media. In practice 'media' stands for editors, reporters, journalists, etc., who deal with public affairs. The lines connecting elements stand for different things: relationships, attitudes and perceptions; one- or two-way channels of communication. There is some correspondence with the Newcomb model (Fig. 2.4.1) in that Elites would be an A, the Public B and the Issues an X. The main differences here are that A and B are now differently motivated role-systems and the element of 'media' has been added as another more or less independent party to the relationship (compare the Westley and MacLean model in the following section).

The model depicts a not uncommon finding of research on public opinion and communication that information about an event or issue is sought from, or acquired by, members of the public, by reference to personal experience, or élite sources, or the mass media, and often from a combination of these. The relevance of theories of interpersonal adjustment and information-seeking just described lies in the fact that the outcome of what is a dynamic situation will depend on the relationships between public and a given élite, on the attitude of the public to the media and on the relationships between élite sources and media channels. Discrepancies between élite and public on issue perception can be a source of strain, leading to attempts to find information from the media and other sources. At the same time, such discrepancies can also lead to attempts by élites to manipulate perceptions by directly acting on events or by trying to control media channels.

The frame of reference established in this way can be enlarged to take account of some variable features of the main elements in the model – élites, media communicators, public and issues. Thus, we can distinguish issues according to their relevance, importance, novelty and controversiality and we can characterize sectors of the public, élite sources of information and mass communicators variously according to their position in the social structure of community or society. In a study of mass media use and opinion about community issues, Tichenor *et al.* (1973) confirmed an initial expectation that the definition of an issue as controversial leads to more learning from the media about that issue. This work was carried out with reference to the existence and development of knowledge gaps (see 4.5) and this approach is particularly relevant to research on convergence and divergence in opinion and information levels between given social groups or categories.

The co-orientation approach is also applicable in public relations (see 7.4), in which case, the public relations agency replaces the media in Fig. 2.4.2 and its client takes the place of an 'élite', in public-opinion terms. The PR agency aims to bring public and client closer together on, for example, some controversial issue like the location of an industrial development. The aim of the agency is to increase awareness of its client's presentation of its stand on the issue and to improve understanding, leading to possible agreement. According to Grunig and Hunt (1984) research shows that use of the the co-orientation model 'Most often improves accuracy, less often improves understanding and least often increases agreement'.

References   **Festinger, L.A.** (1957) *A Theory of Cognitive Dissonance.* New York: Row and Peterson.

Grunig, J.E. and **Hunt, T.T.** (1984) *Managing Public Relations.* New York: Holt, Rinehart and Winston.

Heider, F. (1946) 'Attitudes and cognitive information', *Journal of Psychology,* **21**: 107–12.

Klapper, J.T. (1960) *The Effects of Mass Communication.* New York: Free Press.

McLeod, J.M. and **Chaffee, S.H.** (1973) 'Interpersonal approaches to communication research', *American Behavioral Scientist,* **16**: 469–99.

Newcomb, T. (1953) 'An approach to the study of communicative acts', *Psychological Review,* **60**: 393–404.

Newcomb, T. (1959) 'The study of consensus' in Merton, R.K., Broom, L. and Cottrell, S. (eds), *Sociology Today.* New York: Basic Books.

Tichenor, P.J., Rodenkirchen, J.M., Olien, C.N. and **Donohue, G.A.** (1973) 'Community issues, conflict and public affairs knowledge' in Clarke, P. (ed.), *New Models for Communication Research.* Beverly Hills, CA: Sage Publications.

2.4.3   Theory of consonance and dissonance

An extension of balance and co-orientation theory can be found in the study of public opinion change, where two opposing tendencies have been frequently observed – one towards consensus (convergence of opposed viewpoints), the other towards polarization (divergence). This is sometimes referred to as 'assimilation versus contrast'. The underlying logic and dynamic has been explained above, especially in the context of interpersonal relationships. Research on mass media and public opinion has enabled us to state some of the conditions under which one or other tendency is likely to occur, in particular when people are likely either to distance themselves from media sources (greater dissonance) or to assimilate to media source views (consonance). This process may occur, for instance, in election campaigns, where different media support different parties or candidates.

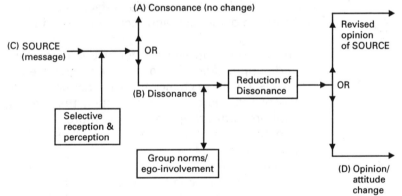

Fig. 2.4.3   Consonance/dissonance and the influence process (adapted from van Cuilenburg and Noomen 1984).

The main features of the process depicted in Fig. 2.4.3 are as follows. First of all, incoming messages are scanned and screened by their receivers, with the general effect of reducing the chance of dissonance (avoiding exposure to unacceptable messages) and maintaining consonance with the environment; situation (A). Because of the inefficiency of this process, or changed circumstances, situations of potential dissonance do arise, where new or contrary opinions are received; situation (B). Dissonance activates the social and psychological processes (especially group norms and ego-involvement) which in turn shape the two main possibilities for restoring balance (the normal or comfortable state of consonance between source and receiver). These are: changing the perception of the source (C) (for instance, finding it less attractive or credible); or changing the opinion or attitude which is at stake (D).

A hypothetical example would arise where a voter in an election reads a newspaper article about a scandal affecting one party leader. Where this refers to a party not supported, consonance is maintained and there is no effect (except perhaps of reinforcement of views). Where the message concerns the voter's own party, loyalty is disturbed. The options for restoring the former consonance are to assert a scepticism about the newspaper source (thus neutralizing the effect of bad news) or to become less inclined to support the party (an opinion and possibly a behavioural effect). The associated factors at work are:

1. Selective perception and reception, which provide an initial screening.
2. Group norms, to which reference is made for reassurance and support for existing opinion. The more supportive the norms, the more chance there is of option (C), revising opinion of the source and discounting the message. The less support from group norms, the more isolated the receiver and the more chance of being influenced in opinion or behaviour.
3. Ego-involvement. The extent to which an opinion represents a deep personal commitment or component of the personality; the more such commitment, the less chance of change and the more chance of rejection of the source and of any disturbing message.
4. Extent of the opinion discrepancy. Research indicates a complex relationship between this and potential responses. Small differences between message and existing position will not generally lead to any change (neither option (C) nor (D) comes into effect); medium differences are likely to require some adjustment, often in the direction of revision of

opinion; large differences usually involve activitation of group norms and ego-involvement and are more likely to cause a rejection of the message and of the source and a reassertion of the opinion allegiance. This has been referred to as a 'boomerang' effect when a message intended to influence has the reverse effect – actually increasing the attitude gap between source and recipient).

Reference van Cuilenburg, J.J. and Noomen, W. (1984) *Communicatiewetenschap.* Amsterdam: Coutinho.

2.4.4 A convergence model

The consonance/dissonance model is especially suited to analysing situations of potential change based on disagreement and conflict. However, much communication takes place under conditions of potential agreement or increasing consensus and consonance and increasing commonality between participants can be considered as one definition of communication. The conflict or propaganda situation represented by an election campaign is not typical. More often, the interests of senders and receivers of messages are potentially consistent, as in many public information or mobilization campaigns (see Ch. 7). According to Rogers (1986, p. 200) 'Communication is a process in which participants create and share information with one another in order to reach a mutual understanding'. This proposition is visualized in Fig. 2.4.4, as follows.

The model depicts the relationship between participant A and participant B in a communicative interaction. There is a cyclical process of moving towards greater mutual understanding based on the giving and receiving of information. Several cycles of information exchange occur before mutual understanding is reached and this does not have to be complete. In this model, the

communication process is presumed to have already begun before we can start to observe it. The cycle develops as follows: A

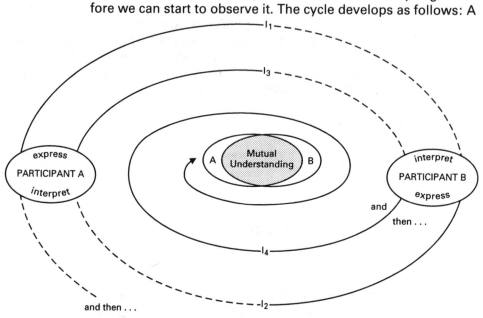

Fig. 2.4.4   A convergence model of communication (Rogers and Kincaid 1981).

seeks to share information (I_1) with B, who perceives, interprets
and responds (I_2); these phases are repeated until there is no
further increment of understanding. The degree of understanding reached is indicated in the figure by the shaded area where A
and B overlap. Convergence is always between two or more
persons. The model, writes Rogers (1986, p. 201), 'compels us to
study differences, similarities and changes in human interrela-
tionships over time'.

This model of communication is argued to have several advantages over the linear one-way model (see above), especially its
emphasis on mutual understanding and consensus, on relationships within networks, which consist of interconnected individuals linked by patterned flows of information which provide
continuous feedback. The model is thought especially suitable
for many situations in developing countries, where culture and
power gaps between senders and receivers have to be bridged

and this can only be achieved by gradual increases of trust and mutual awareness (3.4).

References   **Rogers, E.M.** (1986) *Communication Technology*. New York: Free Press.

Rogers, E.M. and **Kincaid, D.L.** (1981) *Communication Networks: Towards new Paradigms for Research*. New York: Free Press.

2.5   WESTLEY AND MACLEAN'S CONCEPTUAL MODEL FOR COMMUNICATION RESEARCH

This influential model, dating from 1957, was developed with the intention of ordering existing findings of research and providing a systematic treatment which would be especially appropriate for mass communication research. Its origins lie in social psychology and in theories of balance and co-orientation (e.g., Heider 1946: Festinger 1957). Its immediate predecessor lies in the basic model of communicative acts (Newcomb 1953) which was described in the previous section.

Westley and MacLean were concerned to provide a model which represents the much more complex situation of mass communication, while retaining the systematic and interrelated character of the simple case of co-orientation of two persons in relation to external objects.

Westley and MacLean's adaptation of Newcomb's ABX model

The adaptation of the Newcomb model was based on the authors' perception of the main differences between mass communication and interpersonal communication. These differences are:

(a)   the fact that in mass communication the possibilities for feedback are minimized or delayed;

(b)   the larger number of A's (alternative media sources) and X's (objects in the environment) to which a given individual B (as an audience member) must be orientated and amongst which he has to select.

Their model is presented here in two stages.

The basic situation in general communication is represented by a first adaptation of the Newcomb model in the form shown in Fig. 2.5.1.

At this point, the model shows the activity of a source of information, A, selecting from the confusion of X's to communicate with B. In addition, B can have some direct perception of an X

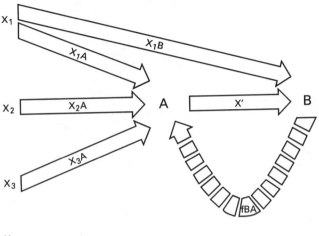

Fig. 2.5.1 First modification of the ABX model, in which A selects from potential X's to communicate with B (Westley and MacLean 1957).

(X B) and can respond, by the feedback link (fBA). This would represent a common case in interpersonal communication, where information is being given by one individual to another or sought by an individual from an expert source.

The second modification (Fig. 2.5.2) involves an additional element, the channel role, C, which stands for the mass communicator. This additional role acts as the 'gatekeeper' for the transmission of messages about the environment between A and B. In this version of the model, A stands for a source in society and B for a member of the society. The channel role is conceived of as having an impartial task of interpreting the needs of B and then satisfying them by transforming meaning into a shared symbol system (encoding) and transmitting messages to B by way of a channel or medium.

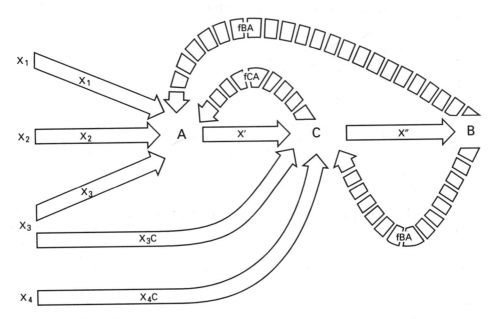

Fig. 2.5.2 Westley and MacLean's conceptual model of mass communication, in which a second type of communicator, C (channel role), is introduced (Westley and MacLean 1957).

The main components of the model can now be described as they correspond to the normal mass communication situation.

X   stands for any event or object in the social environment, about which communication takes place by way of the mass media (for instance, price changes, political crises, election results and so on).

A   is described as an 'advocate' role and refers to the position of individuals or organizations which have something to say about X's to the public as a whole. They might be politicians or advertisers, or news sources. The assumption built into the term 'advocate' is that A's are *purposive* communicators.

C   is the media organization or the individual within it, who selects amongst the A's for access to the channel reaching the audience, according to criteria of perceived relevance to audience interests and needs. They may also select directly amongst the X's for communicating to B (the audience). An implied aspect of the C role is that it serves as an agent of the needs of B, as well as for A. Essentially, this role is *non-purposive*, there is no communicative purpose, except as part of a general aim of satisfying the needs of B.

B   represents the audience or 'behavioural' role and can stand either for individual or group, or even a social system, to which needs for information or orientation to an environment, can be attributed.

X'   is the choice made by the communicator (C) for access to the channel and X" is the message as modified in the media organization for transmission to the audiences.

fBA   is the feedback from member of the public (B) to the original source (A). This might, for instance, be a vote for a political party or a purchase of a product.

fBC   is the feedback from audience member to communication organization, either by way of direct contact, or by means of audience research. Over time this feedback guides future selections and transmissions on the part of C.

fCA   is feedback from communicator to advocate. This may either encourage or modify, or reject the attempt at purposive communication by A.

X_3C etc. stands for observations amongst X's made directly by mass communication organization, for instance an eyewitness account by a reporter.

The model is important for drawing attention to a number of significant and distinctive aspects of the mass communication process:

1. The several stages at which selection takes place: amongst aspects of the environment by 'advocates' who might be experts or genuine opinion leaders; amongst the advocates by the mass communicators; amongst the events or objects of the real world by mass communicators; amongst the

messages transmitted by communicators, on the part of members of the audience.

2. The self-regulating character of the system, arising from the (presumed) diversity of C roles. This should guarantee that the needs of B for relevant messages are met, since competition between C's for attention should ensure that reality is adequately conveyed.

3. The distinction between purposive and non-purposive communication, both of which occur in mass communication. The former is here represented primarily by the advocate role. Where A communicates non-purposively about an X, then A simply becomes another X. In this model, the actions of C are generally thought to be non-purposive, except in sofar as these actions mediate or serve the needs of advocates or audience. Earlier models seem not to allow for the very common circumstance of 'directionless' communication. In this model, the allocation of purpose can be made at either end, as the motives of the audience or those of the would-be communicators.

4. The importance of feedback (or its absence), usually from the audience (B) to either A or C. In the terms of this model, it is feedback which helps to ensure the systematic character of the relationship between participants.

5. The model is intended to illustrate a situation where links between X or A on the one hand and B on the other are not monopolized by one C role. B may have other direct links with A (e.g. through membership of an organization) and may have direct experience of X (e.g. price rise, change in weather).

Applications of the model

The main purpose of the model is to help in posing questions for research about real mass communication situations, and especially about the mass communicator or media organization. For instance, it suggests the following questions. What are the relevant characteristics of those who occupy C roles (the mass communicators)? How independent are C's from each other? What criteria are applied by C in allocating access to either X's or A's?

How adequately are the needs of B interpreted? In what ways are messages about X's altered in passing through the C position in the communication chain? These questions are all fundamental to much research on communicators and their organizations and such research has grown in volume since the model was first published. The model has been cited in several studies of gatekeeping and used in a number of empirical and conceptual studies (e.g. Gieber 1960; Blumler 1970; McNelly 1959).

A good example of the application of the model can be found in Blumler's (1970) analysis of the relationship between politicians, television broadcasters and the electorate in Britain. The advocate (A) role equates with that of the politician who wants to use television (C role) to reach the voters (B role). The situation contains elements of tension because access has to be limited and because there is a potential conflict between broadcasters' wish to please and serve the public and the claims of different political interests over television as a channel to voters. The tension has been increased by the growing importance of television as a means of political communication and the increasing public expectation that television should be not only a channel for political messages, but also a source of criticism, scrutiny or guidance in the public interest. Thus conflict is located mainly in relations between A and C. It is further accentuated in the case of public broadcasting systems by the clash between broadcasters' wish for independence and their formal accountability to the public by way of the political system. The model proved very useful in directing attention to the main points at issue in this case and it could equally provide a useful framework for comparisons over time or between different political systems.

The model is also relevant to situations of planned communication, even if designed for essentially undirected (mass) communication. According to Windahl *et al.* (1991), communication planners need to choose whether to adopt a primarily 'advocate' or 'communicator' channel role. Whichever they choose, they have to be sensitive to the needs of professional media gatekeepers. There is also a danger that a planned communication agency may tend to produce messages designed more to satisfy its employer (an A role) rather than to communicate with the public (the B role).

Comment   Despite its theoretical and practical value, there are some problems with the model which should be noted. Firstly, in its original
presentation, it involved the assumption that such a system of
relationships, like that in the original Newcomb model, would be
self-regulating and mutually beneficial to all participants. It
would balance the interests of senders and receivers, given free
operation. In practice, the relationship of the three main participants is rarely balanced and is not only a communication relationship. There is also a political relationship between A and C,
and therefore sometimes one between C and B. Thus, as we saw
in the example, A may have some power over C and nearly
always C depends to some extent on the A role to supply information without which it cannot operate.

A second main weakness is that the model overemphasizes the
degree of integration of the mass communication process and
the degree to which 'advocates', communicators and audience
share the same view of the process. In practice, each may be
pursuing objectives which have often little to do with each other.
'Advocates' may send messages without really wishing or needing to communicate, communicators can follow organizational
aims of their own and audience members may be mainly spectators of whatever is shown to them, without having 'needs' of a
specific kind which communicators have to meet. The model is
thus idealist and somewhat normative in offering what is essentially a free-market version of the communicator role.

Thirdly, the model overstates the independence of the communicator from society, especially in political matters or those which
concern the interests of the state. For example, Tracey (1977)
suggests that there are different possible forms of interrelation-
ship between the three elements of state/commercial structure;
broadcasting institution; and public. In one version, the first two
elements are assimilated and reflect a tendency by the state or
economic power sources to 'colonize' the broadcasting institution or the 'fourth estate' in general.

References   **Blumler, J.G.** (1970) 'Television and politics' in Halloran, J.D. (ed.), *The Effects of
Television.* London: Panther Books.
Festinger, L.A. (1957) *A Theory of Cognitive Dissonance.* New York: Row and
Peterson.

Gieber, W. (1960) 'Two communicators of the news: a study of the roles of sources and reporters', *Social Forces*, **37**: 76–83.

Heider, F. (1946) 'Attitudes and cognitive information', *Journal of Psychology*, **21**: 107–12.

McNelly, J. (1959) 'Intermediary communicators in the flow of news', *Journalism Quarterly*, **36**: 23–6.

Newcomb, T. (1953) 'An approach to the study of communicative acts', *Psychological Review*, **60**: 393–404.

Tracey, M. (1977) *The Production of Political Television*. London: Routledge and Kegan Paul.

Westley, B.H. and **MacLean, M.** (1957) 'A conceptual model for mass communication research', *Journalism Quarterly*, **34**: 31–8.

Windahl, S., Signitzer, B. and **Olson, J.T.** (1991) *Using Communication Theory*. London: Sage.

2.6 MALETZKE'S MODEL OF THE MASS COMMUNICATION PROCESS

In many communication studies and models, the researchers single out one, maybe two, factors for explaining, for example, certain effects or behaviours. This may lead to the false conclusion that mass communication research problems are best analysed with single- or two-factor explanations. The German scholar Maletzke (1963) offers a quite different perspective with his *Schema des Feldes der Massenkommunikation*. This methodically and thoroughly built up model shows mass communication as a process which is, in social psychological terms very complex, and one in which explanations are more likely to be of a multi- than of a single-factor type.

As the model is relatively complex and fairly hard to survey, we will first discuss separately the elements, which are later brought together in the complete model.

Maletzke builds his model upon the traditional basic elements, communicator, message, medium and receiver. However, between medium and receiver he has noticed two more components. A 'pressure' or 'constraint' from the medium and the receiver's image of the medium.

In the first case we are being acquainted with the fact that different media demand different kinds of adaptation on the part of the receiver. Every medium has its possibilities and limitations, and the characteristics of the medium must be considered as influencing the way the receiver experiences and is affected by the media content. Thus, we do not experience a play in exactly the same way when it is performed on the radio as when it is performed on TV. McLuhan's (1964) often-cited expression 'the medium is the message' may well illustrate how seriously the role of the medium in relation to the receiver is sometimes taken. In this context, Maletzke regards the following medium characteristics as relevant:

(a) the type of perception demanded from the receiver (viewer, reader, etc.);

(b) the extent to which the receiver is bound to the medium

spatially and in time;

(c) the social contexts in which members of the audience receive the media content;

(d) the difference in time between event and consumption of the message about the event, i.e. the degree of simultaneity.

The medium image held by the receiver causes expectations of the media content and may thus be assumed to have an influence on the receiver's choice of content as well as on his/her way of experiencing it and responding to it. The prestige and credibility of the medium are important elements in this image.

The two variables of choice and experience/effect may be seen as important dependent variables or consequences in the process of receiving. Apart from the already mentioned variables of 'medium pressure' or 'medium constraint' and the receiver's image of the medium, some other factors or variables in the model may be labelled as causative or independent in this part of the process.

The receivers' self-image – the individuals' perception of themselves, their roles, attitudes and values create a disposition in receiving communication. Social psychological research has shown, for example, that we tend to reject information that is inconsistent with values we ascribe to ourselves.

The personality structure of the receiver – social psychologists often assume that some categories of persons are more easily influenced than others. It is thus often said that individuals with a low self-esteem are more easily persuaded than others (see, for example, Hovland and Janis 1959). This should hold true, too, in the mass communication process.

The receiver's social context – this factor may refer to the surrounding society, the community where the receiver lives, the groups he/she belongs to as well as the individuals with whom he/she interacts. The significance of the group has been testified to by several students of the communication process. The more the individual accepts being a member of a group, the smaller are the possibilities of influencing his/her attitudes with messages which run contrary to the values of the group.

Maletzke also notes that the creators of opinion, through whom mass media content is usually passed on, are frequently to be found in the receiver's immediate social surroundings, for instance in his local community.

The receiver as a member of the public: the receiving situation is not the same in mass communication as in face-to-face communication. As a member of the unorganized mass public, the individual receiver does not face any great demands to respond or to act in a certain way as he/she does in the less anonymous face-to-face situation. The very situation of receiving may influence the experience. We know, thus, that children experience dramatic mass media content differently if it is consumed together with peers or together with, for example, their parents (Himmelweit *et al.* 1958).

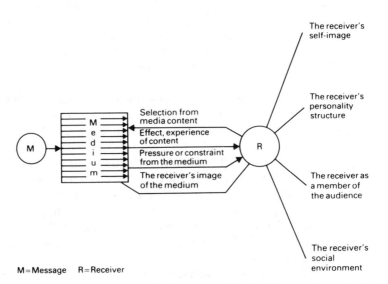

M=Message   R=Receiver

Fig. 2.6.1   The receiver part of the Maletzke model, showing audience behaviour as a result of a number of factors (Maletzke 1963).

So far the Maletzke model may be represented graphically as in Fig. 2.6.1. We have hitherto studied the receiver part of the model. Now let us look at the communicator part of it.

In the same way that we regarded the choice and experience of the receiver as dependent variables, there are two such variables related to the communicator. These are the *communicator's choice to transmit what he/she transmits* and *his/her way of giving shape to the message.* These two may be labelled the communicator's communicating behaviour.

The communicator in the mass communication process has, as a rule, more material or potential messages to start with than he/she will pass on. In such cases the communicator has to sample from the total amount of material according to certain criteria.

When deciding how to structure and give shape to the messages, the communicator is also faced with situations of choice. How the selection and shaping are performed depends among other things on the following factors in the model.

'Pressure' or constraint from the message: the communicator is bound to adapt the shaping of the message to the type of content. A report from a funeral is made differently from a gossip column. A single message may also be regarded as an element of a whole. A news item may be structured in a special way to fit into the whole news programme.

'Pressure' or constraint from the medium: every medium offers the communicator a special combination of constraints and possibilities. The press journalist and a colleague on TV have different conditions to observe in reporting the same event.

The communicator's self-image: this factor does not merely comprise the way the communicator looks upon his/her own role as an individual but also how the role as a communicator is perceived, whether the communicator sees himself/herself as an interpreter of events, a crusader for special ideas or just as a mirror of events, and if he/she thinks that this professional role permits him/her to put forward personal values or not.

The personality structure of the communicator: Maletzke assumes that the personality affects the communicator's behaviour. At the same time he points out that the other dependent variables probably reduce its importance. (For an example where this factor is taken into account, see Swanson 1956.)

The communicator in the working team: the mass communicator seldom works alone, but is dependent on colleagues and specialists around him. This distinguishes for example the journalist from other creators such as novelists. Because of working within a team, the mass communicator's freedom is limited to a certain degree by the norms and values in the working group.

The communicator in the organization: mass media organizations vary as regards size, aims and type of ownership and policies, all of which are important contextual factors for the individual communicator. As for the policies, some students of mass media organizations have noted that the individual journalist may hold beliefs and attitudes contrary to those of the organization, which may force journalists to follow the explicit or implicit rules. However, the communicator/journalist may also have possibilities of getting round them (see for example Breed 1955).

Pressure and constraints caused by the public character of the media content: the fact that the mass media communicator's production is open to inspection by the public puts some constraints, both psychological and legal, on the communicator's work. Often a certain amount of control is exercised by professional associations.

The communicator's social environment: in almost the same way that the social environment of the receiver affects the manner of selecting and experiencing the media content, the communicator's way of gatekeeping and shaping the content is dependent on his/her social surroundings, not only those which the working team and the rest of the organization constitute.

The communicator part of Maletzke's model will look like this graphically (Fig. 2.6.2).

The complete model adds some further relevant factors.

1. The receiver's and the communicator's image of each other: it is often stressed in communications research, that when creating messages, the communicator has a picture of the receiver in mind, even if the latter is not physically present (Fearing 1953). For the mass communicator, a certain problem arises because the audience is often heterogeneous and anonymous, and because the actual existing feedback provides a weak basis for a true and satisfying image of the audience. This circumstance diminishes the effectiveness of the communication.

2. We have already noted that the receiver's image of the medium is important for selection and experience. It is often difficult for the receiver to form a picture of the communicator, but, as is the case in the relation to the medium, the

receiver is assumed to be affected by such a factor as the degree of credibility. It is also of importance whether or not the receiver identifies with the communicator and the communicator's values.

3. Spontaneous feedback from the receiver: the mass communication process is mainly to be regarded as a one-way process, in that it mostly lacks the kind of spontaneous feedback that we find in face-to-face communication. As noted above, this lack is one reason for the communicator's (often) inadequate image of the audience.

As all the elements and factors indicated in the Maletzke model have now been treated, we will show the complete model (Fig. 2.6.3).

Maletzke's image of the mass communicating person – communicator or receiver – is a rather complex one. The behaviour of both communicator and receiver is a function of a large number of factors. This complexity is, no doubt, an important reason why mass communication research has been fairly unsuccessful in explaining and predicting outcomes of the mass communication process.

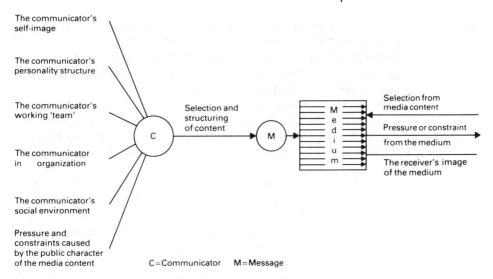

Fig. 2.6.2   The part of the Maletzke model which shows factors influencing communicator behaviour (Maletzke 1963).

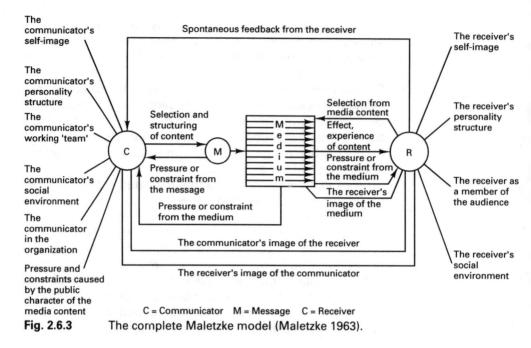

The
communicator's
self-image

The
communicator's
personality
structure

The
communicator's
working 'team'

The
communicator's
social
environment

The
communicator
in the
organization

Pressure and
constraints caused
by the public
character of the
media content

Spontaneous feedback from the receiver

Selection and
structuring
of content

Pressure or
constraint from
the message

Pressure or constraint
from the medium

Selection from
media content

Effect,
experience
of content

Pressure or
constraint from
the medium

The receiver's
image of the
medium

The communicator's image of the receiver

The receiver's image of the communicator

The receiver's
self-image

The receiver's
personality
structure

The receiver as
a member of
the audience

The receiver's
social
environment

C = Communicator   M = Message   C = Receiver

Fig. 2.6.3   The complete Maletzke model (Maletzke 1963).

Comment   The model serves as a summing-up of a couple of decades' social
psychological interest in mass communication. In spite of its
being relatively dated, it is still useful in that it contains a number
of important factors and relationships, some of which have not
yet been very thoroughly studied.

Being so detailed, the model may well serve as a check list of
the relevant factors of the mass communication process, perceived from a social psychological point of view. It may, thus, be
used in cases where one wishes to analyse descriptions of such
processes.

The Maletzke model has been used by the originator himself
when structuring his comprehensive work *Psychologie der Massenkommunikation* (1963), in which every relation, factor and
element is thoroughly discussed. The model also draws attention
to important features of any process of planned communication
(Windahl and Signitzer 1991), especially the need for a communicator to have a clear perception and definition of the intended
audience. The image or perception of the communicator held by

the audience is also very relevant, as is the role adopted by the communicator.

References

Breed, W. (1955) 'Social control in the newsroom: a functional analysis', *Social Forces*, **33**: 326–35.

Fearing, F. (1953) 'Toward a psychological theory of human communication', *Journal of Personality*, **22**: 71–88.

Himmelweit, H, Oppenheim, A.N. and Vance, P. (1958) *Television and the Child*. London: Oxford University Press.

Hovland, C.I. and Janis, I.L. (eds) (1959) *Personality and Persuasibility*. New Haven: Yale University Press.

McLuhan, M. (1964) *Understanding Media*. New York: McGraw-Hill.

Maletzke, G. (1963) *Psychologie der Massenkommunikation*. Hamburg: Verlag Hans Bredow-Institut.

Swanson, G. (1956) 'Agitation through the press: a study of the personalities of publicists', *Public Opinion Quarterly*, **20**: 441–56.

Windahl, S. Signitzer, B., and Olson, J.T. *Using Communication Theory*. London: Sage.

2.7 ALTERNATIVES TO TRANSMISSION: RITUAL AND ATTENTION MODELS

2.7.1 A ritual model of communication

The earliest basic models, as we have seen, took for granted that communication was a linear, one-way, process from source to destination. Advances of thinking led to the recognition of inter-action, feedback and interpretative features in human communi-cation as well as the significance of social context. However, it was James Carey (1975) who first radically challenged the 'trans-mission' or 'transportation' model, of which he wrote: 'the main characteristic is the "transmission of symbols over distance for purposes of control." It implies instrumentality, cause-and-effect relations and one-directional flow. He pointed to the alternative view of communication as 'ritual', according to which 'communi-cation is linked to such terms as sharing, participation, associ-ation, fellowship and the possession of a common faith. . . . A ritual view is not directed towards the extension of messages in space, but the maintenance of society in time; not the act of imparting information but the representation of shared beliefs'. Ritual or expressive communication depends on shared under-standings and emotions. It is celebratory, consummatory and decorative rather than utilitarian in aim and it often requires some element of 'performance' for communication to be real-ized. The message of ritual communication is usually latent and ambiguous, depending on associations and symbols, which are not chosen by the participants, but made available in the culture. Medium and message are usually hard to separate. Ritual com-munication is also relatively timeless and unchanging.

The distinction between ritual and instrumental is one that applies to reception as well as to sending, to 'uses' of communi-cation for the 'audience' as well as aims of would-be communi-cators, although the terms are really inappropriate, since participants take on both roles. The image of the Christmas spruce helps to illustrate a number of these points (Fig. 2.7.1) since, in one culture at least, it symbolizes ideas and values of conviviality, celebration and fellowship which are widely shared and understood, albeit vaguely and variously. There is clearly no instrumental purpose.

In this example, the iconic image of the tree is both medium and (symbolic) message and elements of performance are found in its decoration and display and in associated rituals, for instance of present-giving. In other examples of ritual communication, a series of pre-encoded actions or a text (as in a religious service or a state ceremony) would play a similar part. Although, in natural conditions, ritual communication is not instrumental, it can be said to have consequences for society (e.g., more integration) or for relationships. In some planned campaigns (see Chapter 7) for instance, in politics or advertising, the principles of ritual communication are sometimes taken over and exploited (use of potent symbols, latent appeals to cultural values, tradition, etc.).

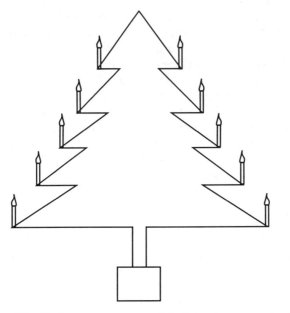

Fig. 2.7.1   The Christmas spruce model of ritual communication.

2.7.2   Communication as display and attention

Besides the transmission and ritual models, there is a third perspective which captures another important element of mass
communication. Often the primary aim of mass media is neither
to transmit particular information nor to unite a public in some
expression of culture, belief or values, but simply to catch and
hold visual or aural attention (McQuail 1987). In doing so, the
media attain one direct economic goal, which is to gain audience
revenue (since attention = consumption, for most practical purposes) and an indirect one, which is to sell (the probability of)
audience attention to advertisers. As Elliott (1972) has pointed
out, mass communication is rarely communication at all, in the
sense of the ordered transfer of meaning. It is more likely to be
'spectatorship' and the media audience is more often a set of
spectators than participants or information receivers. The *fact* of
attention often matters more than the quality of attention (which
can rarely be adequately measured). While those who use mass
media for their own purposes do hope for some effect (e.g.,
persuasion or selling) beyond attention, the latter remains the
immediate goal and is often treated as a measure of success or
failure. A good deal of effort in media production is devoted to
devices for gaining and keeping attention by catching the eye,
arousing emotion, stimulating interest. This is sometimes referred to as a triumph of 'media logic', with the *substance* of a
message often subordinated to the devices for presentation
(Altheide and Snow 1979).

The attention-seeking goal also corresponds with one important perception of the media by their audiences, who use the
mass media for diversion, escape and passing time. They seek to
spend time 'with the media'. The relationship between sender
and receiver according to the attention/display model is not necessarily passive or uninvolved, but it is morally neutral and does
not in itself necessarily involve the transfer or creation of meaning. The process at work is not unlike that of the attraction of
ferrous objects which come within the field of a magnet. As with

magnets, the power of the media to attract is temporary, some-times reversed (repulsion), does not work with everyone and has little long-term effect.

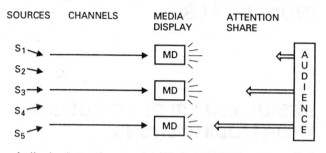

Fig. 2.7.2   A display/attention model (McQuail 1987).

Figure 2.7.2 illustrates the case where several sources (S) employ different and competing media channels to display their messages (MD) (in graphics or sound) with a view to gaining the attention of the same audience 'market'. There is often a zero-sum element built into this situation, in so far as, at any given moment, the attention potential of the available audience is limited, and one channel or display's gain must be another's loss. The success of communication as display is measured by the relative share of the total amount of attention gained. This can be translated by media organizations into higher ratings, higher advertising rates or higher receipts. For the sources it also provides a measure of success (for instance in campaign situations). Competition for attention may also occur *within* a medium (as in a newspaper) as well as *between* media.

References   Altheide, D.L. and **Snow R.P**. (1979) *Media Logic*. Beverly Hills, CA: Sage.
Carey, J. (1975) 'A cultural approach to communication', *Communication*, **2**: 1–22.
Elliott, P. (1972) *The Making of a Television Series*. London: Constable.
McQuail, D. (1987) *Mass Communication Theory*, 2nd edn. London: Sage.

3 PERSONAL INFLUENCE, DIFFUSION AND SHORT-TERM EFFECTS OF MASS COMMUNICATION ON INDIVIDUALS

3.1 STIMULUS–RESPONSE MODELS AND THEIR MODIFICATIONS

Very much, perhaps even most, of mass communication theorizing has dealt with the question of effects. Effects have been of interest for many groups in society, those who want to reach others with their message and therefore want to get the most effective channel to the audience, and those who express fears for the negative impact of media.

The so-called stimulus–response principle has in this context been of great importance. According to this simple model of learning, effects are specific reactions to specific stimuli, so that one can expect and predict a close correspondence between media message and audience reaction. The main elements in this model are: (a) a message (stimulus, S); (b) a receiver (organism, O); and (c) the effect (response, R). Usually, the relations between these elements are demonstrated thus:

$$S \rightarrow O \rightarrow R$$

The images of a hypodermic needle or a 'magic bullet' were used to represent an early but highly influential mass media version of the effect process. Media content was then seen as injected in the veins of the audience, which would react in uniform and predictable ways.

Behind this conception one would find two main ideas:

1. An image of a modern society as consisting of an aggregate of relatively 'atomized' individuals acting according to their personal interests and little constrained by social ties and

constraints.

2. A dominant view of the mass media as engaged in campaigns to mobilize behaviour according to intentions of powerful institutions, whether public or private (advertisers, government bureaucracies, political parties, etc.).

The main features of this 'mass society' stimulus–response model are:

(a) The assumption that messages are prepared and distributed in systematic ways and on a large scale. At the same time, they are 'made available' for attention by many individuals, not directed to particular persons.

(b) The technology of reproduction and neutral distribution is expected to maximize aggregate reception and response.

(c) Little or no account is taken of an intervening social or group structure and a direct contact is made between media campaigner and individual.

(d) All individual recipients of the message are 'equal' in weighting or value – only aggregate numbers count (as voters, consumers, supporters, etc.).

(e) There is an assumption that contact from the media message will be related at some given level of probability to an effect. Thus, contact with the media tends to be equated with some degree of influence from the media, and those not reached are assumed to be unaffected.

DeFleur (1970) has discussed some of the modifications made to the stimulus–response model. One has been called the individual differences theory of mass communication. It implies that media messages contain particular stimulus attributes that have differential interaction with personality characteristics of members of the audience. The revised stimulus–response theory allows for intervening personality variables. Research on propaganda designed to reduce prejudice provides a good illustration of the individual differences theory (Cooper and Jahoda 1947). In this research it turned out that prejudiced people systematically misinterpreted the message of an anti-prejudice cartoon series.

Based primarily on the individual differences theory is the 'psychodynamic model' (DeFleur 1970; Fig. 3.1.1), which rests on the belief that the key to effective persuasion lies in modifying the internal psychological structure of the individual. Through this modification the desired behaviour responses will be achieved.

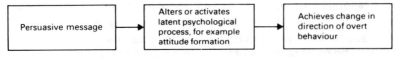

Fig. 3.1.1   DeFleur's psychodynamic model, showing the internal psychological structure as in intervening variable in the effect process (DeFleur 1970).

The research supporting the model includes a wide range of studies of the existence of more or less 'persuasible' types of personality (e.g. Janis and Hovland 1959) and other work on the dispositions of the receiver and attitudes to the source. DeFleur concludes that while the psychodynamic model has not been fully verified, it does seem to work some of the time. Essential to this model is a focus on variables relating to the individual recipient, a retention of the simple cause and effect hypothesis and often a reliance on attitude change as an index of behaviour change.

Comment   Halloran (1969) notes that the 'mechanistic stimulus–response model' is important because 'even in its crudest form it has not entirely disappeared' and 'because it has provided a base from which so much of our thinking about mass communication has stemmed'. This seems to hold true even today, and many researchers blame the stimulus–response principle for having given rise to the notion of the mass communication process merely as a process of persuasion. Another very common accusation relates the exaggerated ideas about the omnipotence of the mass media to the stimulus–response model.

In spite of the criticism levelled at this model, nobody can deny that it directs our interest to an important part of the mass communication process. Knowing today that the early naive versions of stimulus–response theory give a too simple picture of mass communication, we still cannot reject their modified versions as useless and uninformative.

References Cooper, E. and **Jahoda, M.** (1947) 'The evasion of propaganda', *Journal of Psychology*, **23**: 15–25.

DeFleur, M. (1970) *Theories of Mass Communication*. New York: David McKay.

Halloran, J.D. (1969) 'The communicator in mass communication research' in Halmos, P. (ed.), *The Sociology of Mass Media Communicators. The Sociological Review Monograph, 13*. University of Keele.

Janis, I.L. and **Hovland, C.I.** (1959) *Personality and Persuasibility*. New Haven: Yale University Press.

3.2   KATZ AND LAZARSFELD'S TWO-STEP FLOW MODEL OF MASS MEDIA AND PERSONAL INFLUENCE

This model emerged originally from the first rigorous study of the effects of mass communication in an election campaign – the United States presidential election of 1940 (Lazarsfeld *et al.* 1944). The findings failed to identify significant direct effects on voting or opinion from the main media of newspapers and radio and thus undermined widespread assumptions at the time that mass media operated according to the stimulus–response model outlined above. As one explanation of the apparent lack of effect, the authors concluded (p. 151) that 'ideas often flow from radio and print to the opinion leaders and from them to the less active sections of the population'. This is the classic statement of a

Early mass communication model

Two-step flow model

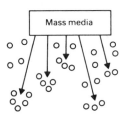
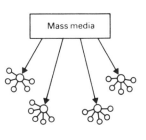

O = Isolated individuals
constituting a mass

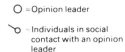

O = Opinion leader

O = Individuals in social
contact with an opinion
leader

Fig. 3.2.1   Two-step flow model of media influence compared with the traditional model of mass communication (derived from theory in Katz and Lazarsfeld 1955).

'two-step' flow of influence. The view that interpersonal influence was stronger than that of mass media gained wider currency following the publication some years later of another study designed to test this proposition in a number of different contexts (including consumer behaviour) (Katz and Lazarsfeld 1955). The result was a very influential body of theory concerning the role of 'opinion leaders' and of 'personal influence', which was later described as a 'dominant paradigm' of communication theory and research (Gitlin 1978). The essence is portrayed in Fig. 3.2.1.

The model of 'two-step flow' involves the following main assumptions:

1.   That individuals are not social isolates, but members of social groups interacting with other people.
2.   That response and reaction to a media message will not be direct and immediate, but mediated through, and influenced by, these social relationships.
3.   That two processes are involved, one of reception and attention and another of response in the form of acceptance or rejection of the influence or information attempt. Reception does not equal response, nor does non-reception equal non-response (because of secondary acceptance from personal contracts).
4.   That individuals are not all equal in the face of media campaigns, but have different roles in the communication process and, in particular, can be divided into those who are active in receiving and passing on ideas from the media and those who mainly rely on other personal contacts as their guides.
5.   That the occupants of the more active role (opinion leaders) are characterized by more use of the mass media, higher levels of gregariousness, a self-perception as influential on others and as having an attributed role as source and guide.

To summarize, according to this model, mass media do not operate in a social vacuum but have an input into a very complex web of social relationships and compete with other sources of ideas, knowledge and power.

While the revised view was welcomed as more realistic and proved a stimulus to research, it was also subject to much criticism and further revision, especially in relation to political communication in modern democratic elections (Kraus and Davis 1976). Aside from the ambiguity of its concepts and lack of any clear empirical demonstration of the two-step process (Lin 1973), the most serious weakness was seen to be its implicit denial or subordination of the original 'one-step' process of influence direct from media to individuals, especially in the age of television. Robinson (1976) revised the model on the basis of election research to take account of the fact that in addition to there being political opinion givers and receivers, there is an even larger category of less attentive 'non-discussants' who may be much open to direct influence from mass media. This leads to the versions of the process shown in Fig. 3.2.2, providing a further update (see Windahl *et al.*, 1991, pp. 56–7).

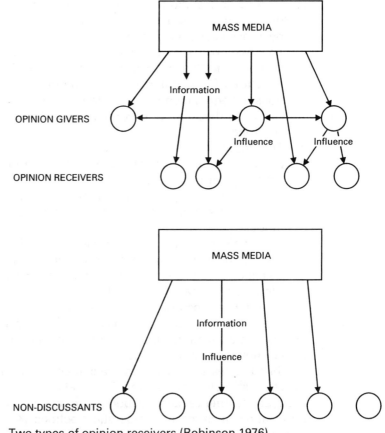

Fig. 3.2.2   Two types of opinion receivers (Robinson 1976).

Robinson (1976) distinguishes between people who are involved in social networks (they get some information from what he calls 'opinion givers') and those who are not so involved, and who are more susceptible to a one-step influence emanating from the mass media. Hence there are at least two types of opinion receiver as shown in Fig. 3.2.2.

Aside from the paucity of empirical verification, several commentators (e.g. Gitlin 1978; Okada 1986) have pointed to the ideological function served by the 'two-step' theory. It expresses a particular and idealized view of individualistic and participative democracy of the American type and it appears to banish the demons of mass society. Despite the many revisions and the criticisms (summarized below) it is clear that the idea of personal influence is an important one for understanding many of the limits and alternatives that still exist to mass communication. In certain areas (e.g., of consumer choice or private behaviour), personal influence is often strong and in certain circumstances (e.g., restricted or untrustworthy mass media) personal contact may have more effect on attitude and behaviour. It is also clear that attention to personal influence is appropriate in more traditional social structures (see 3.4 below).

Comment   We can summarize a few main points to bear in mind concerning this model of media effect.

1. There is no clear or fixed division between the roles of giving and receiving information or influence, and adoption of these roles varies according to topic and circumstances.
2. Opinion 'leaders' and 'followers' may have much in common and differ from a significant third category of 'non-discussants' and non-participants.
3. On many topics, a large number of individuals are directly informed and influenced by mass media, without the intervention of opinion leaders.
4. There are several alternative processes at work, some with 'multiple' stages, as in news or rumour diffusion.
5. Non-media channels are also often at work and can be a primary source of information and influence (e.g., the work organization, trade union, local community, voluntary

association). This possibility reflects the direct contact between A and B roles shown in the Westley–MacLean model
(2.5).

References   **Gitlin, T.** (1978) 'Media sociology: the dominant paradigm', *Theory and Society*, **6**: 205–53.

Katz, E. and **Lazarsfeld, P.F.** (1955) *Personal Influence*. Glencoe: Free Press.

Kraus, S. and **Davis, D.** (1976) *The Effects of Mass Communication on Political Behavior*. University Park, PA: Pennsylvania State University Press.

Lazarsfeld, P.F., Berelson, B. and **Gaudet, H.** (1944) *The People's Choice*. New York: Free Press.

Lin, N. (1973) *The Study of Human Communication*. Indianapolis, IND: Bobbs-Merrill.

Okada, N. (1986) 'The process of mass communication: a review of studies on the two-step flow of communication hypothesis', *Studies of Broadcasting*, **22**, 57–78.

Robinson, J.P. (1976) 'Interpersonal influence in elections campaigns: the two-step flow hypothesis', *Public Opinion Quarterly*, **40**: 304–19.

Windahl, S., Signitzer, B. and **Olson, J.** (1991) *Using Communication Theory*. London: Sage.

3.3   COMSTOCK'S PSYCHOLOGICAL MODEL OF TELEVISION EFFECTS ON INDIVIDUAL BEHAVIOUR

This model (Comstock *et al*. 1978) is an attempt to find an organizing framework for the results of many empirical enquiries into the direct effects of television viewing on behaviour, with particular reference to the influence of dramatic fiction. While the emphasis is also on unplanned and undesirable effects (especially aggression and delinquency), the model could also apply to 'pro-social' influence, information learning, or to the imitation of any behaviour shown on TV. We call this a psychological model because it deals with mental states and with individual learning and behaviour. A main assumption of the model is that television viewing should be treated as a 'functional alternative' for any other personal experience or observation which might have consequences for the individual. Thus, it covers not only cases where TV 'teaches' behaviour, but also where TV provides a stimulus for putting into effect what is learnt from other sources.

The general process depicted in the simplified version of the model (Fig. 3.3.1) can be described as follows. An individual watching a particular TV representation of a behavioural act receives several 'inputs' which may be relevant to his or her own behaviour. The main input will be the portrayal of a specific action (= TV act). Associated inputs will be the degrees of excitement, arousal, attractiveness, interest and motivation which characterize the presentation (together these are labelled 'TV arousal'). In addition, it is likely that alternative actions and forms of behaviour will be represented in the same context (these are labelled 'TV alternatives'). Two other relevant inputs will be the consequences of the action as these are shown on TV ('TV perceived consequences') and the degree of realism in the portrayal ('TV perceived reality'). The central proposition of the model is that a given portrayal of an action is more likely to lead to learning of that action, the more *salient* it is for the individual (i.e. the more psychologically important), the more *arousal* there is and the more *prominent* the action is in the total repertoire of behaviours available to the individual.

Both salience and arousal are necessary conditions for learning, without which the process is negated, while prominence is a matter of degree. The supposition of the model in this respect is that the smaller the repertoire of available acts, that is to say the fewer the alternatives to the specified TV act, the more likely is the latter to be adopted. Finally, we can observe that for a learned act to be actually applied, there must be an opportunity in real life.

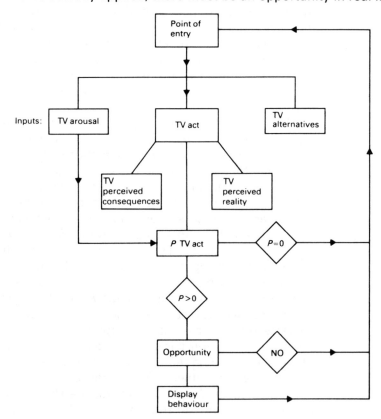

Fig. 3.3.1   A simplified version of Comstock's psychological model of television's effects on individual behaviour (Comstock *et al.* 1978).

The model is given in the form of an 'itinerary' of an individual in time, starting with exposure to a given television portrayal, proceeding through the experience of acting or not acting and returning to a new or repeated television experience. Thus the model stands for one 'loop' in a sequence in which subsequent television experience will be conditioned or modified by earlier viewing and its consequences. In principle, the model portrays the situation of an individual coming to television for the first time, but in the normal case the model relates to one 'moment' amongst others which make up the experience of television.

Definitions of terms in the simplified model

TV act: any form of human behaviour shown on television;
Inputs: messages from television and associated attributes;
TV arousal: extent to which a person is motivated to perform any act in current situation;
TV perceived consequences: sum of all positive, minus all negative, values which are learnt from television and which go with a given act;
TV perceived reality: degree to which a person perceives the television portrayal (TV act) to be true to life;
TV alternatives: other (relevant) social behaviours shown on television;
P TV act: probability of carrying out the TV act;
Opportunity: real-life chance of putting TV act into practice;
Display behaviour: observable performance of social behaviour shown on television.

Dynamic process of the model

1. An individual observes a television portrayal of a social behaviour, together with associated inputs of arousal, perceived consequences of the behaviour and presentations of other related, similar or alternative behaviours.
2. The probability of learning or applying a behaviour shown on TV depends, first of all, on the salience, or psychological importance, of the the act. Salience will be given by three factors: first, the very fact of representation; second, the

degree of positive value attached – the more positive the more salient; third, the degree of realism. As to the first, the authors propose that although demonstration on its own may at first markedly increase salience, after a certain point repeated demonstrations will have diminishing effects.

On the second point, positive valuation depends mainly on the kind of consequence shown to occur for the actor or the community. Indications of moral justification will play a part as well as evidence of personal satisfaction, reward or punishment.

Reality perception is considered to be very important to the model, since the authors interpret research evidence to show that where portrayals are totally dissociated from real life, the act will have no significance for the individual and produce no tendency to learn or apply. Finally, we can conclude that the degree of salience always depends on the prominence of the given act amongst others and this depends both on the number of other acts presented and the relative time and attention paid to the act in question.

3. At this point in the model we can say that the more salient acts are likely to be adopted and non-salient acts are likely to be ignored. Now the amount of arousal plays a critical part. Arousal comes from two main sources: intrinsic property of the presentation and circumstances of viewing and predisposition of the viewer. These are hard to separate empirically, so that it is proposed only that without some arousal of either kind even salient events will have no effect (PTV act $= 0$). Any increment in arousal will increase the probability of a salient act being applied.

4. For acts which emerge with some probability of application, there must still be some opportunity for trial and where none exists, the process is stopped and the viewer 'returns' to the 'loop' of repeated or further viewing.

5. Finally, there can be implementation of the act itself which is open to observation and the viewer is 'returned' to subsequent viewing experiences in a different frame of mind and with altered probabilities for future behaviour.

Examples

We can describe two hypothetical cases to illustrate the model, one in which behaviour was learned and applied and another in which no observable consequences ensued.

In the first example a viewer sees a realistic police story in which the police hero deals brutally with a drug dealer. A physical beating is shown centrally and realistically in an exciting way and the story suggests that it is a justifiable and necessary, even if illegal, way to deal with someone who would otherwise go unpunished. The salience of the act (the beating) is high, alternatives are not shown and there is an opportunity soon after for a given viewer to act roughly in play with friends. From the model, such action would be predicted, since a positive value is given to aggression under conditions favourable to its learning and application in real life.

In the second hypothetical case, a cartoon film shows a witch poisoning a beautiful and good princess. The degree of arousal is high, but the salience of the poisoning act is low, firstly because the episode is unrealistic and secondly because it is an act with evil consequences carried out by an unattractive actor and, perhaps additionally, because the cartoon is full of violent but unlikely incidents (large repertoire). The question of opportunity does not arise since the probability of imitation is already zero.

Comment   Comstock *et al.* tested this model against research evidence relating to aggression, pro-social behaviour, political socialization and erotic arousal, mainly derived from studies of children and adolescents. While the model provided a useful framework it was concluded that at many points the model raises more questions than it answers and there was insufficient evidence either to validate or to reject it. There are obvious weaknesses in a model which abstracts one small part of experience from a large and complex web and which tries to subsume many variables under labels which do not have a precise single meaning. However, in order to carry out experimental research in the psychology of the effect process, some abstraction is unavoidable. The model well

represents a certain way of doing research according to a particular definition of effects and it could help to clarify thinking which
underlies these kinds of research.

Reference   Comstock, G., Chaffee, S., Katzman, N., McCombs, M. and Roberts, D. (1978)
Television and Human Behavior. New York: Columbia University Press.

3.4 ROGERS AND SHOEMAKER'S MODEL OF INNOVATION DIFFUSION

One of the most important applications of mass communication and research has been concerned with the process of encouraging the adoption of innovations. This is relevant both to developing and to more advanced societies, since there is a continuing need, under conditions of social and technological change, to replace old methods by new techniques. It concerns mass communication, since there are many circumstances where potential changes originate in scientific research and public policy which, to be effective, have to be applied by many individuals or small organizations which are outside the direct centralized control of government or large undertakings.

In practice, the targets for most efforts at innovation diffusion have been farmers and members of rural populations. These efforts were first made and evaluated in the United States in the 1920s and 1930s, and are now a feature of most programmes for development in Third World countries. They relate not only to agriculture, but also to health and social and political life. Well before the ideas of interpersonal influence had been formulated and tested in mass communication research (see 3.3), they had been recognized and put into practice by rural sociologists and change agents (Katz 1960).

For the student of mass communication models, the most important features about work on diffusion are: the weight which has to be given to non-media (often personal) sources (neighbours, experts, etc.); the existence often of a campaign situation in which behavioural changes are sought by giving information and trying to influence motivations and attitudes. Because of the large amount of empirical research on diffusion (much of it summarized in Rogers and Shoemaker 1973), the model which has emerged is a much tested one, although it is limited to a set of rather specific circumstances.

The model chosen to illustrate this approach (Fig. 3.4.1) is taken from Rogers and Shoemaker (1973) and is based on the assumption that there are at least four distinct steps in an 'innovation-diffusion' process:

Knowledge: the individual is exposed to an awareness of the existence of the innovation and gains some understanding of how it functions.

Persuasion: the individual forms a favourable or unfavourable attitude towards the innovation.

Decision: the individual engages in activities which lead to a choice to adopt or reject the innovation.

Confirmation: the individual seeks reinforcement for the innovation decision he or she has made, but may reverse the previous decision if exposed to conflicting messages about the innovation.

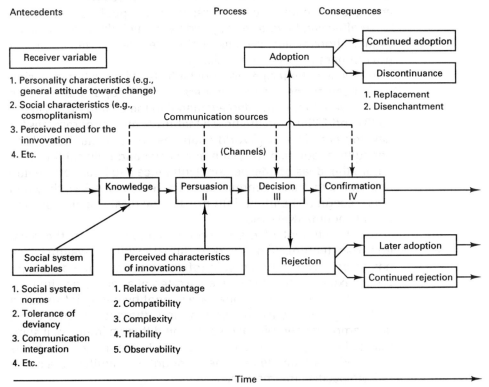

Fig. 3.4.1 Rogers and Shoemaker's paradigm of the innovation-diffusion process, indicating the four steps of knowledge, persuasion, decision and confirmation (Rogers and Shoemaker 1973).

This model incorporates the following ideas about the diffusion process:

1. It distinguishes the three main stages of the whole event into *antecedents, process* and *consequences.* The first of these refers to those circumstances of the event or characteristics of the people involved which make it more or less likely that an individual will either be exposed to information about an innovation or will experience needs to which the information is relevant. For instance, innovation adoption is more likely to occur amongst those who are well-disposed towards change, appreciate the need for innovation and who look out for new information. The *process* is one of learning, attitude change and decision. Here the perceived characteristics of the innovation play a major part, as do the norms and values of the relevant social system. Sometimes technically efficacious means may be unacceptable on moral or cultural grounds or may present a threat to the existing structure of social relations. The stage of *consequences* of the diffusion event is mainly taken to refer to the later history of use or disuse, if adoption takes place.

2. There is a need to separate out the distinct functions of 'knowledge', 'persuasion', 'decision' and 'confirmation', which must normally occur in this sequence, even if the sequence need not be completed. Different kinds of communication process may also be involved in each case. For instance, the characteristics associated with early persuasibility or persuasiveness. The early knowers are not necessarily the opinion leaders and indeed there is some reason to believe, on the basis of research evidence, that early knowledge can go with a degree of social isolation, just as can a lack of knowledge. A lack of social integration may be related either to being 'in advance' of society or to a 'lagging behind'.

3. Diffusion of innovation will normally involve different communication sources – general mass media, advertising or promotional material, official agencies of change, informal social contacts – and different sources may be important at different stages and for different functions. Thus mass media and advertising may produce awareness and knowledge, official agencies at the local level may persuade, personal

influence may be important for the decision to adopt or not and experience of use may provide a main later source of confirmation or otherwise.

4. The model shows 'receiver variables' to apply at the first or 'knowledge' step, since the acquisition will depend on personality, social characteristics, etc. However, at least some of the receiver variables will be just as important at subsequent steps in the process. The same applies to 'social system variables' which are also related to the knowledge step in the model, but which may be influential later.

Rogers (1986) has applied the model to the case of new communication technologies (e.g., personal computers or videotex) and points to some distinctive features. Firstly, there is the question of reaching the 'critical mass' of adopters of an interactive communication technology. This represents a threshold beyond which the benefits for new adopters are accelerated. In general, a higher rate of actual adoption helps to make an innovation 'normal'. Secondly, the new media are 'tool technologies' rather than ends in themselves. Adoption and implementation depends on *re-invention* to suit particular needs. Thirdly, adoption (acquisition) as such is less significant than continued implementation and use. This case is also a reminder that different types of innovation may involve different types and sequences of innovation process.

Comment   The model is a distillation of a large amount of experience in the applications of mass media and other agents for purposes of planned change. It is also an outcome of much past research. Even so, it is a prescriptive model in many respects and involves a number of assumptions about an ideal way of proceeding which may not always fit actual conditions and may be open to criticism on normative grounds. The model represents a 'dominant paradigm' of the relation between communication and development which some believe to be outmoded. The main author of the model, E.M. Rogers, has himself described the passing of this dominant paradigm (Rogers 1976) and has criticisms of the approach which are consistent with some of our comments.

1. The model is designed from the perspective of an external or

superior agent of change, which decides what is beneficial (on technical grounds) and proceeds to promote it by mobilizing large resources. Against this, it can be said that change can and should occur from *below* by those who need it on their own behalf. The more this is done, the less relevant is the model presented.

2. The model presupposes a linear, rational sequence of events, planned in advance and with criteria of rationality determined externally. This is a common correlate of the external or manipulative approach just mentioned.

3. In the model, persuasion or attitude change is located between 'knowledge' and 'decision'. This need not necessarily be the case. There are other bases for decision-making than the formation of a judgemental attitude and there is much debate about the notion that attitude change normally precedes a related behaviour change. Often the latter is itself a major *cause* of attitude adjustment.

4. In real life there is much randomness and many elements of chance in decision-making. It is possible that an innovation may be adopted with little knowledge or for prestige, or in imitation of another, etc.

5. The model would be more complete if it included certain feedback loops from later to earlier steps. Thus decision-making and confirmation feedback to knowledge and attitude can increase or reinforce these respectively.

6. Different types of innovation may involve different processes of diffusion.

References   Katz, E. (1960) 'Communication research and the image of society', *American Journal of Sociology*, **65**: 435–40.

Rogers, E.M. (1976) 'Communication and development: the passing of a dominant paradigm', *Communication Research*, **3**: 213–40.

Rogers, E.M. (1986) *Communication Technologies*. New York: Free Press.

Rogers, E.M. and Shoemaker, F. (1973) *Communication of Innovations*. Glencoe: Free Press.

3.5   NEWS DIFFUSION

The term diffusion is also used in another branch of communication research – that relating to the spread of information amongst a population, especially as a result of mass media news. Interest has centred on the speed with which news is diffused, the relative effectiveness of different media channels and the part still played by person-to-person communication in an age of mass communication. Some of the theory developed in relation to innovation diffusion also applies to the case of news.

3.5.1   The 'normal' diffusion curve

It has been long noted that the curve for diffusion of innovations and of information often takes an S-shaped form. In the earliest phase only a few people are 'adopters' or 'knowers' and the cumulative curve builds up slowly, then accelerates, subsequently levelling off, when saturation is approached and few additional adopters or knowers are added per unit of time. According to Chaffee (1977) this 'normal' pattern is not so much an empirical finding of research (though it is often empirically observed) as a hypothetical norm or standard which can be used in research. The pattern is not, for example, likely to be found in its complete form in relation to typical items of news information. Deviations from the normal pattern can, nevertheless, be used to identify factors which facilitate or constrain diffusion. Chaffee points to three main kinds of deviation: (A), the frequent case of incomplete diffusion, where less than 100 per cent of a population is reached; (B), a much more rapid acceleration at the start than is normal; or (C), a much slower rate of acceleration. These are illustrated in Fig. 3.5.1, which represents the 'normal' (or random model) curve and the three deviant types.

These three kinds of deviation can, in general, be accounted for by constraints either on the sender or on the receiver side, or by

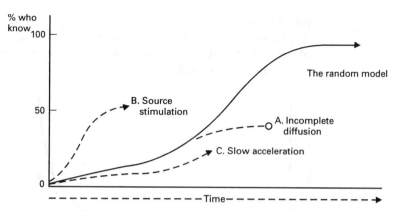

Fig. 3.5.1   The 'normal' curve of information diffusion and three deviant types (Chaffee 1977).

topic-specific limitations (news topics vary in the probability of 'normal' learning or awareness effects). For example, 'sender-side' constraints would include failure to give sufficient or continuing attention to a topic leading to a slow or incomplete diffusion (A or C). 'Receiver-side' constraints include lack of background knowledge, news interest or processing skills (also leading to A or C). Regarding topic-related factors, it is obvious that some news events are of deeper, wider or more enduring interest than others and can also 'develop' as news stories at quite varied paces (resulting in pattern B or C). News of an earthquake or an assassination is likely, for instance, to show a much more accelerated diffusion pattern (type B) than, say, economic news. This opens up a large field of research in which account should be taken at the same time of the media and the supply of information as well as of the audience and its level of knowledge or awareness of news events.

3.5.2   The J-curve model

In this section, we focus on one aspect of the interaction between media channels and audience in the diffusion process; the part played by interpersonal channels in the information. It turns out that the type of subject matter (rather than just varying topics) plays a key role in determining the path of diffusion, and a quite different curve (the J-curve) better represents the process of interpersonal diffusion of news.

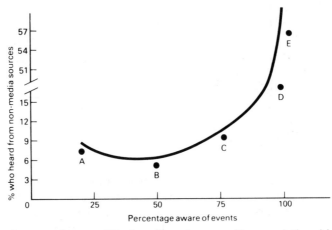

Fig. 3.5.2   J-curve of news diffusion: there is a curvilinear relationship between the proportion aware of an event and the proportion who heard from a non-media source (Greenberg 1964).

Much attention was given to the role of person-to-person news diffusion immediately following the Kennedy assassination in 1963 (e.g. Greenberg 1964; Schramm 1971) because of a special concern with the need to control public reaction and avoid panic. There had already been research into the sources of knowledge of news events (Larsen and Hill 1954; Deutschman and Danielson 1960) with particular reference to comparisons between the mass media and personal contacts. The model discussed here grew out of this earlier work, but comes most directly from Greenberg's work on the Kennedy assassination. The J-curve (Fig. 3.5.2) which was used to illustrate and summarize the findings of research *is not itself a model* but it reflects the outcome of a particular process which can be put into model form (Fig. 3.5.3).

Greenberg set out to test a proposition, based on the earlier work, to the effect that events reported in the news can be classified into three groups, according to the degree of personal diffusion they are likely to receive:

Type I: Events which are of low general importance, but of great significance to a few. Such events will not get prominent treatment in the media, but since knowledge of the events is important to a certain target or reference group, they are likely to be selectively noticed by some of the relevant minority and news of them passed on to others who did not happen to see the first announcement. Ultimately, all or most of the relevant group are likely to have some knowledge of the events, but a rather high proportion will have heard through a personal intermediary. An example might be the press publication of national examination results, where the relevant public consists mainly of friends and relatives of the candidates.

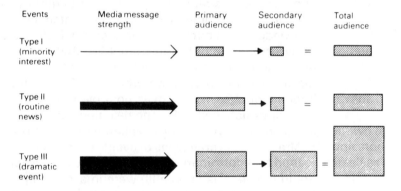

Fig. 3.5.3   Diffusion model underlying the J-curve, showing the relationship between types of event and primary, secondary and total audiences.

Type II: Events which are agreed to be of general public importance (the normal main news stories of the day), which get a fair degree of prominence in the media and are noticed directly by a majority or large minority of the general public. Such stories are not likely to be passed on as information from person to person (although they might be discussed), partly because they can be assumed to be known, partly because they are not usually sufficiently dramatic or immediate to merit personal volunteering of the fact to some other person. Such events might include the settlement of a major strike, a planned rise in train fares, a large bank robbery, a terrorist outrage somewhere else in the world, etc.

Type III: Events of extreme urgency, importance and high dramatic quality which are sure eventually to come to the attention of almost everyone and which get very high and rapid media attention. The classic case is the Kennedy assassination itself. Paradoxically, however, despite the enormous media attention, we can expect the *proportion* of those eventually having the information who heard it first from another person will actually be a good deal higher than in the previous category of main news stories. The significance of the event mobilizes both interpersonal and media communication channels.

The J-curve illustrated in Fig. 3.5.2 is a summary of the results obtained by Greenberg when he investigated the first sources of knowledge of 18 different news events, which ranged in degree of eventual total diffusion from 14 to 100 per cent. When the proportion of people ultimately aware of these events was plotted against the proportion who heard about them first from interpersonal sources, it was possible to group them into five categories (labelled A–E). The resulting curve took on a J-shape in accordance with the proposition outlined below.

Although the three types of events described above and represented in the summary research findings (A is in type I; B, C and D are in type II; E is in type III) were in ascending order of actual diffusion, as plotted along the horizontal axis, the proportion who heard from personal sources (vertical axis) does not increase progressively and is not related in a linear way. The proportion hearing from personal sources is *rather low* for events of low total awareness, *very low* for most events of 'medium awareness' and then very high; (more than 50 per cent) for events of maximum awareness.

The underlying process which produces this J-shape can be expressed in Fig. 3.5.3. The model shows, for different types of events, the relative share of total audience attributable to personal contact. Type I refers to news items of low general importance, but which are very relevant to a special minority. Type II are average general news stories. Type III refers to events of very high significance. The total audience reached increases progressively, but the relative share of the secondary (personal contact) audience in the total audience does not. It is higher for type I than for type II and highest of all for type III.

Comment
1. The model points to the distinction between the 'importance' of events and the degree of attention or involvement by a given group of people. 'Importance' is related to general news values in a society and the salience of an event for society as a whole, while relative involvement is associated with high personal salience for the individual receiver. The two are not directly correlated since high involvement can go with events which have no general social importance.
2. The model and the research on which it is based remind us that most events which are covered in the mass media and subsequently known about by a section of the public are learned *first* from the media and not from personal sources.
3. It appears that type III events, where much knowledge comes from personal sources, are rare and likely to be associated with crisis situations. We can remark as a further distinguishing feature of such events, that they are also likely to be very *rapidly* diffused and come to a *maximum* awareness more quickly than other news events come to *partial* awareness.
4. We know from studies of crisis and rumour (e.g. Shibutani 1966) that the processes outlined by the model can be influenced by unusual conditions, especially conditions of deprivation or attenuation of media sources, in which uncertainty leads to much more active seeking for information from non-media sources.
5. The model lends itself to a wider application than the situation discussed here, since it could help to distinguish between news events of different kinds (e.g. sports results, foreign stories, political events) and between different minority publics amongst the general audience.

References
Chaffee, S. (1977) 'The Diffusion of Political Information' in Chaffee S. (ed.), *Political Communication*. Beverly Hills, CA: Sage.
Deutschmann, P.J. and **Danielson, W.A.** (1960) 'Diffusion of knowledge of a major news story', *Journalism Quarterly*, **37**: 345–55.

Greenberg, B.S. (1964) 'Person-to-person communication in the diffusion of news events', *Journalism Quarterly*, **41**: 489–94.

Greenberg, B.S. and **Parker, E.B.** (eds) (1965) *The Kennedy Assassination and the American Public*. Stanford, CA: Stanford University Press.

Larsen, O. and **Hill, R.J.** (1954) 'Mass media and interpersonal communication in the diffusion of a news event', *American Sociological Review*, **19**: 426–33.

Schramm, W. (1971) in Schramm, W. and Roberts, D. (eds), *The Process and Effects of Mass Communication*. Urbana: University of Illinois Press.

Shibutani, T. (1966) *Improvised News*. New York: Bobbs Merrill.

3.6 NEWS COMPREHENSION, PROCESSING AND RECALL

As mass media have come to occupy a more central place in political and social processes there has been an increased focus on the news, which is for most people the main means of access to political participation. It is also via the news that governments, parties and interest groups seek to exercise power and influence. This line of thinking assumes that news is an informative, credible and effective means of communication and a good deal of research has been devoted to testing this assumption. Television news has been a particular object of research given the fact that a few national television channels often dominate as the channels of public communication. Mass mediated news is a distinctive form of informational communication, with the following general features:

- news is rarely 'purposeful' communication (news services are usually information 'brokers' trying to match the needs of suppliers and consumers of news) (2.5);
- public attention is always voluntary;
- attention is also often unspecific, guided by a wide range of motives or simply a general one of environmental 'surveillance';
- much of the information provided is perishable and always changing from day to day.

Because of these features, we may expect little cumulative learning from news and what is learnt is often not applied in everyday life. News media are not usually regarded as public educators and the criteria of success or effectiveness applied to the news informational process are usually limited to two matters: the degree of audience attention received; and the degree to which news is understood by its audience. The three main measures applied in news effect research are:

1. the extent of audience *reach;*
2. audience *recall* of news content;
3. audience *comprehension* of particular items of news.

One further, and important, consequence of the features noted above is that news communicaton has to be viewed as a process of selection, reception and processing by the news receiver as much as one of transmission by a news sender. This has consequences for the choice of model for portraying the news process and explains why two versions are offered – one a model of *transmisson*, another of *processing* (and interpretation) by the receiver. Whichever of these two perspectives we choose, news communication involves a sequential process. At any given moment in the process, there will be influences from many antecedent and contextual factors.

3.6.1   A transmission model of news learning

In the 'transmission' version, the main emphasis is on the factors and conditions which are associated with news recall and 'comprehension' by the audience, according to the intention of the original source or sender. The form of the model is derived from that of Comstock *et al.* (1978) (3.3 above) and shown in Fig. 3.6.1.

The sequence depicted – from news source to conclusion of a potential cycle of learning – involves several stages, with a set of different factors at work at each stage.

Stages 1–2. From display to exposure: The probability of reaching an audience depends on both 'sender-side' (message) and 'receiver-side' (audience) variables (see 3.5). In respect of the former, news is more likely to receive attention if it is perceived as interesting (scores high on news values), is given prominent presentation and treatment and is carried by high audience channels at favourable times. The perceived status of a channel will also affect the probability of attention-giving. On the receiver side, individuals are more likely to attend to news if they have a 'news habit', belong to social-demographic groups with high news-use tendencies (e.g., older and better-educated people, men more than women) and are already well-informed about related news issues.

Stage 3. Processing: The probability of a particular item being 'processed' by a receiver as potential information depends on two main factors: its being affectively arousing and attention-gaining; its being selected as relevant or interesting. Many news items which are recorded as reaching an audience (see Fig. 5.4.1) may be scanned without registering any cognitive or emotional effect. Audience reach or attention may be recorded, without any process of interpretation taking place. Items which are not processed cannot be comprehended or have learning effects.

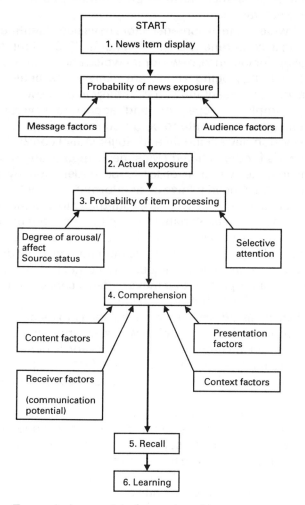

Fig. 3.6.1   Transmission model of news learning.

Stage 4. Comprehension: This generally refers to the ability to attribute a meaning to items in line with the intention of the sender (but see 3.6.2 and 5.3). It can rarely be directly or fully measured, only indicated in approximate ways. The probability, degree and quality of comprehension, in the sense defined, are dependent on four main kinds of variable relating to: item content or substance; form of presentation; context of reception; receiver variables.

A wide range of content factors have been identified as contributing to comprehension (see Trenaman 1967; Robinson and Levy 1986). For instance, news topics which are concrete and personal, other things being equal, are likely to be better understood. Factors of presentation are less easy to pin down, although clarity, simplicity, repetition and appeal to several senses are thought to contribute to comprehension. From their studies of television news, Findahl and Hoijer (1984) concluded that 'most news is for the initiated'. Most news reports are fragmented and incomplete, while in order to be understood by the average person they need to give clear information about the causes and effects of events as well as about the who and the where.

Many 'receiver' variables also play a part, but the more important appear to be previous interest in and knowledge about a topic, plus general 'communication potential', as determined by education and social milieu. The context of reception plays a more minor part, but whatever affects concentration and attention also affects comprehension.

Stage 5. Recall: This refers to the ability to recognize or correctly reproduce the content of news. Measurement can take several forms and the time interval can also vary. In general, recall varies differentially according to the same factors as those which relate to comprehension, although the two can be measured independently.

Stage 6. Learning: This notional outcome of news exposure and processing presumes some longer-term residue of information which feeds back to subsequent news-seeking and processing behaviour. For it to be further explored, reference has to be made to the 'receiver-side' model of news comprehension which follows. In general, any significant 'effect' of news belongs under this heading and it is the culmination of the cycle of attention, processing, comprehension and ability to recall.

3.6.2   Processing the news – a reception model

As seen by the audience, 'news' forms a very large and continuing supply of very disparate information, most of which passes us by completely or is noted with minimal interest or understanding. We are very inefficient as well as very selective 'consumers' of news. Nevertheless, it is clear from research as well as everyday experience that both the selection and sense made of news follow some consistent patterns. This has been underlined by those who have studied audience motivations for attending to news (e.g. Levy 1978) or response to news information (e.g. Robinson and Levy 1986).

News research has shown that much news is presented within frameworks of meaning which derive from the way in which news gathering and processing is organized and from the need to present news in a way which aids audience understanding. The 'framing' of news within thematic and topic categories also reflects the contexts and purposes of the sources in society which supply news to the media in the first place. Newspapers and news bulletins are organized in consistent and easily recognizable sections differentiated by topic and format (e.g., information about events, editorial comment, background features). An experienced 'news user' learns the relevant category system which is an indispensable aid to 'following' the news.

These remarks connect with another body of communication research and theory which relates to processes of selection, perception, 'decoding' and 'meaning-construction', which most people apply to their everyday experience and to their encounters with incoming sensory information of all kinds (see 5.3). Out of the two streams has been derived a 'frame theory' of news (owing something also to Irving Goffman), according to which individuals can be thought of as applying 'frames' or 'schemata' to new information in order to make sense of it and relate it to what they already know.

Such interpretative frames or schemas have been described by Anderson (1980) as 'large, complex units of knowledge that organize much of what we know about general categories of objects, classes of events and types of people'. They provide guides to cognition, valuation and location of new items of information. Usually they are collectively constructed and widely shared within a society, community or social group. The broadest and most enduring have a national or international currency, but many alternative and overlapping interpretative frames are also available. Examples of global frames of meaning include the 'Cold War', 'Third World poverty and dependence', 'Threats to world environment', 'Nuclear holocaust'. At a national level, common frames of interpretation are provided by and for issues of economic welfare, party political conflict, national sporting achievement, etc.

Such schemata provide classificatory schemes, guides to selection, relevance and significance and make it much easier to avoid as well as to seek and make sense of information. Most relevant here is the part they play in the understanding of news, as indicated by Schank and Abelson (1977). There is still not a great deal of evidence concerning the actual shape and distribution of interpretative frameworks amongst people. The indications are that the schemata 'in people's minds' are much more diverse, fragmentary, inconsistent and poorly organized than the theory supposes. Even so, there is enough evidence and commonsense support to suggest that a process following the lines shown in Fig. 3.6.2 is often at work in audience news processing. The model is a simplified version of Axelrod's (1973) 'Schema theory: processing model of perception and cognition', as described by Graber (1984).

The conditions for attention indicated in Fig. 3.6.1 are assumed to have been met for any significant processing to occur. Alternative sequences can be followed requiring more or less effort and leading to more or less learning ('success' or 'failure'). The two main cognitive activities involved are: 'matching' new information with old (pre-existing) frames; checking new and unorganized information with old items of information. The logic of the model indicates a few basic sequences, as follows.

Sequence A (1–2–3–9–11) is a common and 'successful' path to

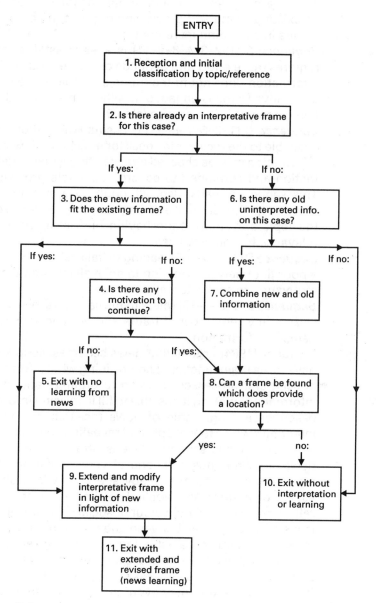

Fig. 3.6.2   Schema theory news processing model (adapted from Graber 1984).

news learning. An item of information is readily perceived to fit an existing frame and processing requires minor extension and results in a learning increment.

Sequence B (1–2–3–4–8–9–11) is a 'successful' strategy which requires more effort and depends on some motivation; the new information does not fit the frame available and a search for an alternative frame is engaged in. Where this is found, a modified and extended frame ensues (step 9).

Sequence C (1–2–6–7–8–9–11) occurs where there is no frame available to the receiver to check for matching. However, the new information may be checked against other isolated items of information and combined to construct a viable provisional frame. This sequence leads also, although by a still more laborious route, to the 'successful' exit. Logically this sequence depends on the topic and information having high salience and potential relevance for the news user.

Sequence D (1–2–3–4–5) leading to 'failure' and exit, results from a poor fit of new information to an available frame and a lack of motivation to seek alternative routes.

Sequence E (1–2–6–10) refers to the case of received information lacking any remembered frame and not connecting with other items of information.

Graber (1984) argues that news schemas, scripts and frames have three main functions: determining what information will be noticed and processed; helping to organize and evaluate new information; making it possible to fill in missing information. She describes a programme of news research involving in-depth interviews with a few people and revealing some of the strategies involved in using schemas. One is 'straight matching', where a news story reminds someone of very similar and typical past news stories. Another strategy she calls a 'spinoff', where an aspect of a story was applied to the future or some general reflection on human behaviour or social events. Thirdly 'comparisons' were employed between one situation in the news in order to evaluate some other situation, possibly closer to home.

It is clear that different people follow quite different, unpredictable and even illogical processing strategies and that concepts of 'success' or 'failure' may even be inappropriate to apply to the diverse and creative ways in which news information is received.

The formalization of the process, as shown in Fig. 3.6.2, is therefore misleading in its rationality and consistency.

Despite some evidence to show the usefulness of schema theory as an orientation to the understanding of news understanding and the intuitive appeal of the approach, it has also been criticized. Woodall (1986) warns against relying too much on the approach. She reminds us that the schema concept has no agreed definition and little is known about it. Not all news stories fit into standardized and stereotyped categories and genuinely *new* information may require quite different kinds of cognitive response. Amongst the many uncertainties about the schema approach is the fact that it is very difficult to know or discover when and if schemas are actually employed in processing by receivers of news, even if the news is often *offered* in schematized forms and seems to end up in people's heads in some similar form of cognitive information.

Despite the emphasis on *reception*, this approach still tends to presume that 'appropriate' interpretation will follow the logic which is built into news by its producers. However, news can be more or less 'open' or 'closed' in terms of the possible meanings to be derived (Schlesinger *et al.* 1983). Research into differential decoding of news (e.g. Morley 1980) also shows that news is often variably interpreted and that news which is not 'understood as sent' does not necessarily fail to be informative (see also Section 5.3 below).

References   Anderson, J. (1980) *Cognitive Psychology and its Implications.* San Francisco: W.H. Freeman.

Axelrod, R. (1973) '"Schema Theory" an information processing model of perception and cognition', *American Political Science Review,* **67**: 1248–66.

Comstock, G., Chaffee, S., Katzman, N., McCombs, M. and Roberts, D. (1978) *Television and Human Behaviour.* New York: Columbia University Press.

Findahl, O. and Höijer, B. (1984) *Begriplighetsanalys.* Lund: Studentlitteratur.

Graber, D. (1984) *Processing the News.* New York: Longman Inc.

Levy, M. (1978) 'The audience experience with television news', *Journalism Monographs.*

Morley, D. (1980) *The 'Nationwide' Audience: Structure and Decoding.* B.F.I. Monographs, London

Robinson, J. and Levy, M. (1986) *The Main Source.* Beverly Hills, CA: Sage.

Schank, R.C. and Abelson, R.P. (1977) *Scripts, Plans, Goals and Understanding.* Hillsdale, NJ: L.E.A.

Schlesinger, P., Murdock, J. and **Elliott, P.** (1983) *Televising Terrorism*. London: Comedia/Marion Boyars.

Trenaman, J.S.M. (1967) *Communication and Comprehension*. London: Longman.

Woodall, G. (1986) 'Information processing theory and TV news' in Robinson and Levy, op. cit., pp. 133–58.

3.7 THE MYCELIUM MODEL OF PUBLIC OPINION AND INTERPERSONAL COMMUNICATION

The 'rediscovery' of the group and of interpersonal influence led to some quite fundamental rethinking about the concept of mass communication. It was even suggested that we should consider mass media communication as a flow *from* people before it is a flow *to* people. Brouwer (1967) provided a rationale and a model

(Public opinion expressed in mass media)

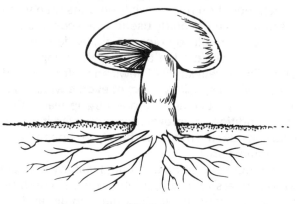

Mycelium

(Network of interpersonal relations)

Fig. 3.7.1 The mycelium model of public opinion (based on theory in Brouwer 1967).

to support this view (Fig. 3.7.1). He drew an analogy between the formation and expression of public opinion (for instance in the mass media) and the growth of mushrooms which, under certain conditions, rapidly make their appearance. In fact, the fungus visible above the ground is a unit of a much more extensive, more enduring and hidden network of fibres (the mycelium) which feed the growth of fungi, which are the fruit of the mycelium. The mass media can be considered as fungi, whose mycelium or roots are the networks of interpersonal relation and discussion which find their visible expression from time to time in the media. In this view, opinions expressed in the media are an *outcome*, not a *cause*, of interpersonal communication networks.

Brouwer emphasized three main assumptions on which this model is based:

1. In mass communication, all communicatory units belong to the same interconnected system (thus individuals in a network as well as mass media 'voices').
2. Specialized units of a communication system (e.g. mass media) are an outgrowth or result of the other units, rather than a cause or precondition. If cut off, they will be replaced by other specialist units.
3. The characteristics of specialist units (mass media) are more dependent on non-specialized units than vice versa.

This model is particularly useful when considering media effects in relation to public opinion which, by definition, has to have its origin and principal life amongst the people who constitute a public. For certain kinds of news and information the model may also be valid, especially news of events which may be known by community participants before they appear in the media. Under some conditions of information, however, it will not be appropriate to consider the media as the expression rather than initiator of communication.

The model has some additional validity in relation to rumour. Rumour refers to informal interpersonal communication which spreads by word of mouth, often rapidly and under particular conditions (Shibutani 1966). These conditions are, especially: sudden good or bad news of high salience and significance; crisis or danger; uncertainty and shortage of reliable information. In these circumstances, the very active interpersonal networks of communication lead to a variety of abnormal, spontaneous and non-institutionalized phenomena such as: formation of 'milling' and restless crowds; demonstrations; manifest collective panic behaviour, such as flight. These may be considered the equivalent of the mushrooms which spring up temporarily and as evidence of the underlying conditions of enhanced and unregulated interpersonal communication. They are symptoms and expressions of disturbed and overactive communication networks.

References   **Brouwer, M.** (1967) 'Prolegomena to a theory of mass communication', pp. 227–36 in Thayer, L., (ed.), *Communication*. London: Macmillan.
Shibutani, T. (1966) *Improvised News*. New York: Bobbs-Merrill.

EFFECTS OF MASS COMMUNICATION ON CULTURE AND SOCIETY

During more than a generation of active research into the effects of mass media, there have, inevitably, been important developments in thinking about the effect process. Here we deal with processes which go beyond those envisaged in DeFleur's 'psychodynamic' model (3.1 above), although we should note that DeFleur had already taken the process somewhat further by speaking of a 'cultural norms' theory of media effect. According to this theory, the media do not only act directly on individuals, but also affect the culture, the stock of knowledge, the norms and values of a society. They make available a set of images, ideas and evaluations from which audience members can draw in choosing their own lines of behaviour.

For example, in the sphere of personal sexual behaviour, the mass media provide cumulatively and often unintentionally a view of what is normal and of what is approved or disapproved. This view may then be incorporated by individuals into their own conceptions of what is either normal or correct. As another example of influence on a social attitude, the mass media seem to provide, on matters of race relations, a relatively homogeneous 'definition of the situation' or statement of the 'problem' and an impression of majority opinion which then helps to shape the response of individuals to specific questions and events.

The transition in thought represented by the difference between a psychodynamic model on the one hand and a cultural norms theory on the other, corresponds quite closely to the distinction between the models discussed in the last chapter and those which follow in this. Until now, the effect processes we have dealt with have exhibited one or more of the following characteristics: the effects are mainly those intended by the senders; they are short term (i.e. immediate and temporary); they have to do with attitudinal, informational or behavioural changes in individuals; they are relatively unmediated.

In this chapter, we are mainly concerned with effect processes which are more unplanned, long-term, indirect and collective. Our attention is directed less at separate 'messages' or items of information than at whole sets or systems of messages which share some features in common. We refer mainly to matters of informational consensus and of ideology in society. Attention is also given to the ties which integrate society or, alternatively, to the forces which tend towards conflict and fragmentation.

4.1 CULTURAL INDICATORS AND THE CULTIVATION PROCESS

One of the most productive and influential traditions of research into the longer-term and indirect effects of the media has been practised under the heading of 'cultural indicators' and 'cultivation analysis'. The origins of the tradition lie in early theories of the great power of the medium of television to shape beliefs, ideas and, indirectly, behaviour. Television was seen as the great storyteller, eclipsing traditional socializing institutions of religion, family and community in industrial mass societies. According to Morgan and Signorielli (1990) 'Cultivation analysis is the third component of a research paradigm called "Cultural Indicators" that investigates (1) the institutional processes underlying the production of media content, (2) images in media content, and (3) relationships between exposure to television's message and audience beliefs and behaviors' (p. 15).

The central hypothesis of the research was that viewing television gradually leads to the adoption of beliefs about the nature of the social world which conform to the stereotyped, distorted and very selective view of reality as portrayed in a systematic way in television fiction and news. Cultivation is said to differ from a direct stimulus–response–effect process mainly because of its gradual and cumulative character. It is also seen as an interactive process between messages and audiences. There are two main underlying assumptions (Gerbner *et al.* 1979). One is that (commercial) television presents an 'organically composed total world of interrelated stories (both drama and news) produced to the same set of market specifications'. Secondly, 'television audiences (unlike those for other media) view largely unselectively. . . . Television viewing is a ritual, almost like religion, except that it is attended to more regularly.'

In this theory of media effect, television provides many people with a consistent and near total symbolic environment which supplies norms for conduct and beliefs about a wide range of real-life situations. It is not a window on or reflection of the world, but a world in itself. The resulting research (led from the

Annenberg School of Communication at the University of Pennsylvania) has had two main wings – one directed to testing the assumption about the consistency (and distortion) of the television 'message system', the other designed to test, by way of survey analysis, a variety of public beliefs about social reality, especially ones which can be tested against empirical indicators. The core of the ensuing analysis is the comparison between beliefs about reality with actual reality, taking account of varying degrees of habitual exposure to television. Those who watch increasing amounts of television are predicted to show increasing deviance of beliefs about reality away from the known picture of the social world and towards the 'television' picture of the world. A major focus of cultivation research has always been on the television portrayal of violence and crime, compared to the actual incidence of crime in society. Other topics of political and social concern have also been studied in a similar way.

In an extensive review of numerous studies into the television construction of reality, Hawkins and Pingree (1983) find many scattered indications of the expected relationships, although they do not find conclusive proof of the *direction* of the relationship between television viewing and ideas about social reality. They say that 'television *can* teach about social reality and that the relationship between viewing and social reality may be reciprocal: Television viewing causes a social reality to be constructed in a certain way, but this construction of social reality may also direct viewing behavior.' The same researchers have also offered a version of the process of cultivation as they see it, in the form of a model, reproduced in Fig. 4.1.1, which identifies some of the variables which research has shown to play a part.

The two chief moments in the potential 'cultivation' sequence are those of 'learning' and 'construction'. For the posited effects to be possible, learning (albeit incidental) has to occur and factors relevant to learning have to play a part. At the learning stages, a range of skills (capacity) are likely to play a part, sometimes differently in relation to other factors such as age. Secondly, the ability to focus on central rather than on incidental information (more likely to be stereotyped) could hold back the posited cultivation effects. Thirdly, degree of attention, indicating relatively active or passive viewing of television can be important – the less attentive and less active, the more likely will be incidental learning and acculturation by television. Fourthly, involvement can play a part especially according to the view that 'low-involvement' facilitates certain kinds of learning and influence (see Section 7.3 below).

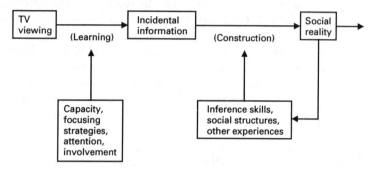

Fig. 4.1.1   A model of conditions in cultivation (Hawkins and Pingree 1983).

At the stage of 'construction' of social reality, the most important determinants of adoption of the 'television view' of the social world are likely to be personal experience and the social structures of family, peer group and the wider community. As to the first, it is clear that personal experience and observation is a source of information about social reality which may either confirm or disconfirm the television image. Social group membership is also likely to vary in the extent to which it supports or challenges the holding of a distorted or limited view. The more consistent and coherent the support from the immediate social environment towards or away from the 'television view' of the world, the more influence on the individual.

Research into the cultivation process has been somewhat limited by its assumptions about the contents of television and the nature of television viewing. The television experience is probably more differentiated and non-cumulative than allowed for in the theory (especially outside the USA) and may be becoming more so as production and supply increases. The relative failure to confirm cultivation effects in cultures other than the United States suggests that the initial hypotheses of the approach were too general. Developments of thinking concerning the active construction of meaning by individuals and the diminished 'power of the text' (see Chapter 5) also undermine the assumption of the long-term cumulative effect of powerful 'message systems'. Even so, it is clear that the line of enquiry represented by cultural indicators and cultivation research is not a spent force and can lend itself to more specified and nuanced enquiries on particular topics. Morgan and Signorielli (1990) identify several critical issues for future research into cultivation, including the following:

- How does cultivation take place?
- What demographic subgroups are likely to be affected?
- What is the role of personal experience in cultivation?
- How do attitudes towards television influence cultivation?
- What is the role of specific programmes and genres?
- How do media other than television cultivate?
- What will be the effect of new technologies on cultivation?

References   Gerbner, G., Gross, L., Morgan, M., Signorielli, N.** and **Jackson-Beek, M.** (1979) 'The demonstration of power: violence profile No. 10.' *Journal of Communication*, **29**, 3: 177–96.

Hawkins, R.P. and **Pingree S.** (1983) 'Television's influence on social reality', pp. 53–76 in Wartella, E., Whitney, D.C. and Windahl, S. (eds), *Mass Communication Review Yearbook*, vol. 5. Beverly Hills, CA: Sage Publications.

Morgan, M. and **Signorielli, N.** (1990) *Cultivation Analysis*. Newbury Park, CA: Sage Publications.

4.2   AGENDA SETTING

Amongst the several hypotheses about the effects of mass communication, one that has survived and even flourished in recent
years, has held that the mass media simply by the fact of paying
attention to some issues and neglecting others will have an effect
on public opinion. People will tend to know about those things
which the mass media deal with and adopt the order of priority
assigned to different issues.

This hypothesis would seem to have escaped the doubts which
early empirical research cast on almost any notion of powerful
mass media effects, mainly because it deals primarily with learning and not with attitude change or directly with opinion change.
Empirical studies of mass communication had in fact confirmed
that the most likely effects to occur would be on matters of
information. The agenda-setting hypothesis offers a way of connecting this finding with the possibility of opinion effects, since
what is basically proposed is a learning function from the media.
People learn what the issues are and how they are ordered in
importance.

The best known of the more recent proponents of the agenda-
setting hypothesis are the American researchers Malcolm
McCombs and Donald Shaw (1972, 1976). They wrote (1976)
'Audiences not only learn about public issues and other matters
through the media, they also learn how much importance to
attach to an issue or topic from the emphasis the mass media
place upon it. For example, in reflecting what candidates are
saying during a campaign, the mass media apparently determine
the important issues. In other words, the mass media set the
"agenda" of the campaign. This ability to affect cognitive change
among individuals is one of the most important aspects of the
power of mass communication.'

It has been the case that most 'agenda-setting' research has
concerned itself with election campaigns. In the typical modern
election campaign it has become a common strategy to establish
the 'image' of a given candidate by association with certain
positions on the perennial problems of a society and with certain

special issues of the candidate's choice. The theory is that if voters can be convinced that an issue is important, they will vote for the candidate or party which has been projected as most competent to deal with it.

4.2.1   The basic model

In addition to its relevance for the practice of political campaigning, the hypothesis has the advantage of appealing to common sense and of seeming relatively easy to test. As shown in Fig. 4.2.1, the basic idea is that, amongst a given range of issues or topics, those which get more media attention will grow in their familiarity and perceived importance over a period of time, and those which get less will decline correspondingly. It should be possible to test this expectation by comparing the results of quantitative media content analysis with changes in public opinion as measured by surveys at two or more points in time.

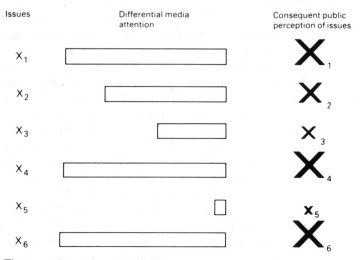

Fig. 4.2.1   The agenda-setting model: matters given most attention in the media will be perceived as the most important.

McCombs and Shaw (1976) take the Watergate affair as an

illustration of the agenda-setting function. There was nothing new in uncovering political corruption, but the intense press exposure and the televised US senate hearings that followed, made it the topic of the year. Nevertheless, the detailed evidence from research has not always confirmed the existence of a powerful agenda-setting process (Becker 1982). The authors of the model report some confirmatory evidence, but others (e.g. McLeod *et al.* 1974) warn against an 'uncritical acceptance of agenda-setting as a broad and unqualified media effect'.

Comment

Some of the uncertainty about the hypothesis stems from unresolved problems in the underlying theory. It is not, for example, always clear whether we should look for direct effects from the media on the personal agendas of individual members of the audience or whether we can expect agenda-setting to work through interpersonal influence. This makes quite a lot of difference to research and to the extent to which we can rely on content analysis to provide an indication in itself of likely agenda-setting effects.

A second problem has to do with the different kind of agendas which are involved. We can speak of the agendas of individuals and groups or we can speak of the agendas of institutions – political parties and governments. There is an important distinction between the notion of setting personal agendas by communication directly to the public and of setting an institutional agenda by influencing the politicians and decision-makers. We can expect the media to have a multiple role in that they may try to influence the opinion of the public and they may also try to influence the élite. In reality there is a continuous interaction between élite proposals and public views, with the media acting as carrier as well as source (see Fig. 2.4.2).

A third theoretical ambiguity concerns the degree of intention which may be attributed to the media. At times, agenda-setting has to be regarded as a more or less conscious and systematic process of attention directing by the media, but at other times agenda-setting theory is closely associated with a functional approach. Thus, according to Shaw (1979) 'Agenda-setting theory of media effects is indebted to this [uses and gratifications] research tradition for its starting points: an initial focus on people's needs.' There is, consequently, some uncertainty about whether agenda-setting is initiated by the media or by the members of the public and their needs, or, we might add, by institutional élites who act as sources for the media.

It would seem that agenda-setting theory has a number of boundaries with other approaches discussed elsewhere in this book and that these boundaries are not clearly marked. It has affinities with the position of Noelle-Neumann (4.4 below), the uses and gratifications approach (5.1), and the news diffusion model (3.5).

If we wish to retain agenda-setting as a theory and a guide to research it may be better to rest it on a combination of socialization and learning theory. Thus, we develop expectations about what are reliable, expert sources of information (the main mass media), we experience situations in which knowledge and judgement about public matters is expected of us and we acquire the means to meet these expectations by learning from the media.

Reese (1991) argues that an important and neglected variable in the process is that of *power*. The relative power of sources in relation to the media and to other sources partly determines *whose* agenda receives prominence.

4.2.2   Rogers and Dearing's model of differential agenda-setting

A thorough review of research findings by Rogers and Dearing (1987) has led to a clearer statement of the *different* agenda-setting processes which are in question and to a more definitive conclusion about the amount and kinds of effect that have been shown. While the simple version of the agenda-setting hypothesis as stated by Cohen (1963) posits an effect from the media on the topics of public opinion, later research has pointed to more complex interactions. Consequently, Rogers and Dearing distinguish between three different kinds of agenda: the *media-agenda*, which refers to the priorities of attention in media content to issues and events; the *public agenda* – the varying salience of issues in public opinion and knowledge; the *policy-agenda*, which describes the issue and policy proposals of politicians. Research appears to show the following main kinds of interactions or effects:

1. Mass media do influence the public agenda directly, presumably by weight of attention and media authority.
2. The public agenda (public opinion) influences the policy agenda, as politicians seek to respond to what voters might want.
3. The media agenda also has independent direct influence on the policy agenda, since it is used by politicians as a guide to public opinion.
4. On some issues, the policy agenda has a direct and strong influence on the media agenda.
5. The media agenda is directly influenced by many sources and by 'real-world events' which come to the attention of the media a factor not usually included in the earlier considerations of the process.

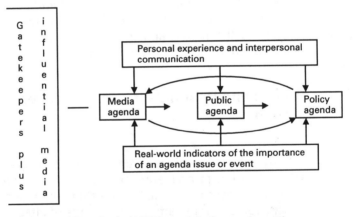

Fig. 4.2.2   Rogers and Dearing's (1987) model of agenda-setting.

This last topic has been given thorough attention by Reese (1991), with particular reference to the balance of power between media and powerful sources. These generalizations can be put together, as in Fig. 4.2.2, so as to show the overall process at work.

The model represents the different kinds of effect and of feedback just outlined. It reminds us, in addition, that mass media, the public and élite policy-makers all inhabit more or less the same wider environment when it comes to highly significant events and that each of the three separate worlds indicated are connected and permeated by networks of personal contacts and influenced by personal experience.

Inspection of the model makes it very clear why most research has been ultimately inconclusive, since it is virtually impossible to identify all the relevant variables or to hold them constant in examining the media effect. Agenda-setting can be intentional or unintentional and it can be initiated by either the media or policy-makers. We cannot exclude the possibility that the public itself affects the media agenda, since some media look for content selection clues in their estimation of current public concerns, independently of events, other media or élite views.

Rogers and Dearing mention some additional sources of variation and uncertainty. One is that media vary in their credibility, so that not all media are equal in their likely effect. Another is that media messages may not coincide with personal experience from the environment. Thirdly, many people may hold different values concerning news events from those which mass media tend to share.

Despite the continuing weak status of agenda-setting theory, Rogers and Dearing are positive about its future and recommend that in future more account should be taken of indicators of 'real-world' events (e.g., Iyengar and Kinder 1987) and of a wider range of issues. They also think that more connections should be made between agenda-setting and other fields of media theory and research. For instance, amongst the topics covered in this book, there are obvious parallels with the uses and gratifications approach (5.1), theories of news comprehension (3.6) and of information diffusion (3.5 and 4.5), the spiral of silence theory (4.4) and dependency theory (4.3), to name the most obvious.

References   Becker, L. (1982) 'The mass media and citizen assessment of issue importance', pp. 521–36 in Whitney C. and Wartella E. (eds), *Mass Communication Review Yearbook*, vol. 3. Beverly Hills, CA: Sage.

Cohen, B.C. (1963) *The Press and Foreign Policy.* Princteon, NJ: Princeton University Press.

Iyengar, S. and **Kinder D.R.** (1987) *News that Matters: Agenda-setting and Priming in a Television Age.* Chicago: University of Chicago Press.

McCleod, J.M., Becker, L.B. and **Byrnes, J.E.** (1974) 'Another look at the agenda-setting function of the press', *Communication Research,* **1,2**: 131–66.

McCombs, M.E and **Shaw, D.L** (1972) 'The agenda-setting function of mass media', *Public Opinion Quarterly,* **36**: 176–87.

McCombs, M.E. and **Shaw, D.L.** (1976) 'Structuring the "Unseen Environment"', *Journal of Communication,* Spring: 18–22.

Reese S.D. (1991) 'Setting the media's agenda: a power balance perspective' in Anderson J. (ed.), *Communication Yearbook 14,* pp. 309–40.

Rogers E.M. and **Dearing J.W.** (1987) 'Agenda-setting research: where has it been, where is it going?' in *Communication Yearbook 11,* pp. 555–94.

Shaw, E.F. (1979) 'Agenda-setting and mass communication theory', *Gazette,* xxv, **2**: 96–105.

4.3 A DEPENDENCY MODEL OF MASS COMMUNICATION EFFECTS

The dependency model has been developed in several versions since its first publication. The most recent variant (DeFleur and Ball-Rokeach 1989) still has as its main focus the relationship between mass media system and social system. The kind and degree of effects which can be expected from the mass media vary according to this relationship. The theory assumes that in a modern (mass) society, the media can be considered as 'information systems vitally involved in maintenance, change and conflict processes at the societal as well as the group and individual levels of social action. The most important and original idea in the theory is that in such a society individuals come increasingly to depend on mass media information for knowledge of and orientation to what is happening in their own society. The kind and degree of this dependency will vary according to two main conditions: the degree to which a society is undergoing change, conflict or instability; and the degree to which the media are in fact central and important as an information source.

4.3.1 The dependency state

The first model, depicted in Fig. 4.3.1, shows the interrelation between three main elements (media, society and audience) and the link with effects.

The model shows the three main elements to be interrelated, although the precise nature of this relationship can vary from one society to another and each separate element can vary in ways which are relevant to the potential for effects on the audience. On the first point, we can simply note that some societies have close control over their media systems, while in other societies the media may have more power to influence society independently. Media can also be related in different ways to their audiences, sometimes following and reflecting, at other times (or in other

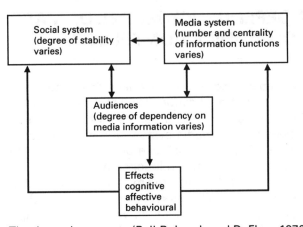

Fig. 4.3.1   The dependency state (Ball-Rokeach and DeFleur 1976).

places) playing a more leading or controlling role. Of the other variations we can say:

- The *social system* varies according to its degree of stability. It can be firmly established, subject to periodic temporary upheavals and internal crises, or it may be weak and in continuing change and uncertainly (as with some developing countries). It may even be in a state of collapse (under conditions of war, revolution or economic ruin). The more change, crisis and uncertainty the more need for information, orientation, definitions, value reassertions, or new value expressions, which stimulate information-giving and receiving. Under these conditions, audiences are more dependent on whatever information systems are available.

- The *media system* can be more or less developed, diverse and capable of responding to the needs of the social system and the audience. The more it has these qualities, the more it is likely to be central to society and the more audiences will depend on it. There may, however, be alternative resources provided by informal or specialized networks or even by communications from outside the society, in which case audience dependency will be lower.

- The *audience* will vary internally according to its dependency on media. Elite social groups are likely to have alternative channels, as may some non-élite minorities. There will also be differences in social composition related to the structure and change of society.

4.3.2   The dependency effect process

While model 4.3.1 relates to the general *structural* conditions of interdependency between media, audience and society, the authors of the model have also developed a *process* model of how

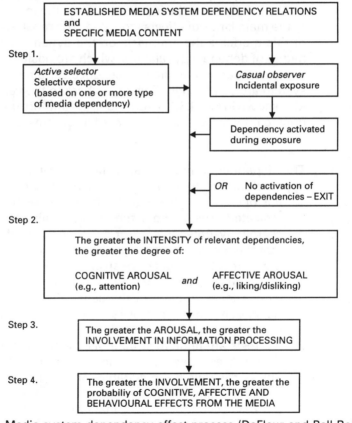

Fig. 4.3.2   Media system dependency effect process (DeFleur and Ball-Rokeach 1989).

dependency works for individual audience members in relation to media, as shown in Fig. 4.3.2. This has some relation to 'uses and gratifications' theories discussed in the following Chapter.

The process depicted is based on a cognitive–rational model, which assumes a logical connection between overt media content and the motives for attention. In the sequence depicted, an active media user chooses particular content, based on a pre-existing dependency (need). The non-selective, casual member of the audience may be caught up and have motives activated, or may leave the process. At Step 2, the more intense the need or dependency experienced, the more cognitive and affective the arousal, the greater the involvement and the more chance of any of the main kinds of effects indicated. The most essential feature of this model is the emphasis on the dynamic and cumulative nature of dependency relations which are posited between audience member and media source, once certain conditions of the system are established. This refers back to the variable possibilities shown in Fig. 4.3.1. This model, the authors point out, relates only to effects from particular media contents on individuals.

Comment   The dependency model has a number of advantages as an approach to the study of general media effects.
1. It is open to a wide range of effect possibilities, as has been indicated. The authors themselves claim that it 'avoids a seemingly untenable all-or-none position of saying either that the media have no significant impact on people or society, or that the media have an unbounded capacity to manipulate people and society'. We may refer to this as a 'contingency' model, in the sense that any given effect is dependent on a more or less unique set of circumstances which hold in a given situation.
2. It directs attention to structural conditions and historical circumstances rather than to individual and personality variables. It is thus more suitable for dealing with sociological questions than most other overall communication models.
3. It takes account of the fact that effects on the audience may also lead to effects on the social system and on the media system itself. Thus it can happen that experience of media

performance may lead to demands for change or reform of the media, to be carried out either through the political system, or by the free market mechanism, by the emergence of alternative media.

A weakness of the model is that it overstates the real independence of the different elements and especially of the media system from the social system. The former tends to be presented as if it were a neutral 'non-political' source available to meet whatever 'need' might arise. It is more likely that a media system will be quite closely associated with, or even incorporated into the dominant institutions of society.

References   Ball-Rokeach, S. and DeFleur, M.L. (1976) 'A dependency model of mass media effects', *Communication Research*, **3**: 3–21.

DeFleur, M.L. and Ball-Rokeach, S. (1989) *Theories of Mass Communication*, 5th edn. New York: Longman.

4.4 THE SPIRAL OF SILENCE

This concept is derived from a larger theory of public opinion which has been developed and tested by Elisabeth Noelle-Neumann over a number of years (1974; 1984; 1991). The 'spiral of silence' refers to only one principle of this body of theory, although it is the one which is of most importance for mass communication. In general terms, the theory of the spiral of silence concerns the interplay between four elements: mass communication; interpersonal communication and social relations; the individual expression of opinion; and the perception which individuals have of the surrounding 'climate of opinion' in their social environment. The theory derives from fundamental social-psychological thinking (Allport 1937) concerning the dependence of personal opinion on what others (are perceived to) think.

Noelle-Neumann (1991) has stated the main assumptions of the theory as follows:
1. Society threatens deviant individuals with isolation.
2. Individuals experience fear of isolation continuously.
3. This fear of isolation causes individuals to try to assess the climate of opinion at all times.
4. The results of this estimate affect behaviour in public, especially the open expression or concealment of opinions.

She adds that this fourth assumption connects all the preceding ones and between them they are 'considered responsible for the formation, defense and alteration of public opinion'. Basically what the theory proposes is that, in order to avoid isolation on important public issues (like political party support), many people look to their environment for clues about what the dominant opinion is and which views are gaining strength or are in decline. If one believes one's own personal views are amongst those in decline, one is less inclined to express them openly. As a result, the views perceived to be dominant appear to gain even more ground and alternatives decline further. Noelle-Neumann (1974) put it as follows:

The more individuals perceive these tendencies and adapt their views accordingly, the more one faction appears to dominate and others to be on the downgrade. Thus the tendency of the one to speak up and the other to be silent starts off a spiralling process which increasingly establishes one's opinion as the prevailing one.

4.4.1   The basic model

The mass media, along with the interpersonal network are the two most important factors in shaping the individual perception of the dominant 'climate of opinion' (what is the prevailing majority view). As Noelle-Neumann (1991) writes:

> assessment of the climate of opinion derives from two sources: immediate observation by individuals in their own spheres of life and indirect observation through the eyes of the mass media. If a certain view predominates in the mass media, this will result in an overestimate of this point of view.

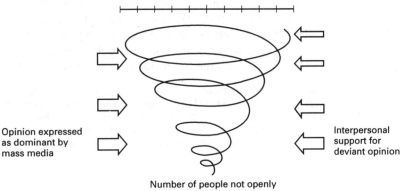

Opinion expressed as dominant by mass media

Interpersonal support for deviant opinion

Number of people not openly expressing deviant opinion and/or changing from deviant to dominant opinion

Fig. 4.4.1   An example of a spiral of silence: mass media expressing dominant opinion together with an increasing lack of interpersonal support for deviant views bring about a spiral of silence, with an increasing number of individuals either expressing the dominant opinion or failing to express deviant ones (based on theory in Noelle-Neumann 1974).

The theory was first formulated to explain puzzling findings in German politics, where polls reported the main parties consistently equal, although at the same time popular *expectations* about which was likely to win increasingly favoured one of the parties, which did in fact then win a very convincing victory. Clearly the expressed voting intentions were concealing some underlying reality of opinion, which many voters were unwilling to express openly and directly. The theoretical interpretation offered, following the principles outlined, was that many people, fearing isolation, looked to the mass media for clues about the dominant opinion. They found strong support in the media for one party (the Social Democrats) although it was actually less popular than the media were indicating. This misperception of the real state of opinion has, in social science literature, been called 'pluralistic ignorance'.

A more recent and different test of the theory in Germany concerned the issue of nuclear energy. Noelle-Neumann (1991) found evidence of growing press attention to the issue between 1965 and 1985, accompanied by a steady decline in the *tenor* of coverage – towards a more negative assessment. Until 1981 a majority of the public was in favour of nuclear energy, but gradually began to lag behind opponents in public opinion measures. Separate measures showed the beleaguered supporters of nuclear energy to face a strong threat of isolation. She comments:

the tenor of the media . . . precedes a change in assessing the climate of opinion [which in turn] precedes a change in one's own attitudes. Behavior – the willingness to speak up – adjusts to the assessment of the climate of opinion, but also, conversely, influences assessments of the climate of opinion, in a process of interaction that creates a spiral.

4.4.2   Process model for individual opinion

There have been a good many attempts to test the theory or to use it to explain other relevant findings of opinion research, with varying degrees of confirmation or uncertainty. One such test

(Taylor 1982), based on a model of stages in the spiralling process, is depicted in Fig. 4.4.2. The main variables included in the model are four in number:

1. One's own opinion on an issue, which can coincide either with the actual minority or the majority view.
2. Perception of the predominant position, which can be either correct or incorrect.
3. Assessment of the future trend, which can favour either the actual minority or the actual majority.
4. Willingness or not to *express* one's opinion (see variable 1).

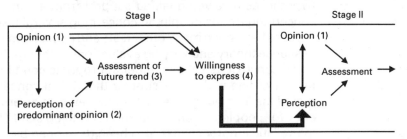

Fig. 4.4.2   Stages and models for individual opinion (Taylor 1982).

In the process model depicted, one's own opinion (1) and perception of what is the dominant opinion (2), are assumed to be related (mutually interactive, hence the double-headed arrow). These two variables are then both assumed to influence judgement of the future course of opinion (3). According to the spiral of silence theory, the fourth variable (willingness to express opinion) (4) depends on an interaction between one's own opinion and perception of the future trend. For those who actually favour the majority position, willingness to express is greater for those who perceive a trend towards greater support for that position. For those who favour the minority position, willingness to express is greater for those who perceive the reverse. Then, according to Taylor's interpretation, the 'spiral' effect comes about because the amount of support that is shown for an opinion affects the public's perception of the strength or predominance of that opinion at some later stage in the development of public opinion. In Fig. 4.4.2 we see stage I and the start of stage II, in what is a continuing multi-stage evolution. The heavy arrow connecting stages I and II represents the cumulative effect of individual changes in probabilities of self-expression on the aggregate mixture of public opinion. In turn, this is the stimulus for an individual's perception of public opinion in the second stage of the process.

Taylor went on to test two hypotheses: one, that those who believe that there is a trend in support of their position are more likely than those who do not to express their opinion; and, two, that those who perceive majority support for their position are more likely than those who do not to express their opinions. Both hypotheses received qualifed support from an analysis of data concerning trends in opinion concerning several issues.

There have been many other tests and applications of the spiral of silence theory and varying evaluations, although few doubt its significance or its validity under appropriate conditions. It is not far out of line with other simpler theoretical concepts, such as that of the 'bandwagon' effect, which refers to an empirical tendency for people to want to be on the winning side. The theory of 'pluralistic ignorance' has also been developed by Scheff (1967) to refer to situations in which many individuals fail to communicate private opinions to each other and come to feel that they belong to a dissenting minority. In fact the majority of individuals may all privately hold the same view, while allowing a powerful and vocal minority to impose a false consensus. The idea of a 'silent majority' refers to a similar phenomenon. Some recent commentators (e.g., Csikszentmihalyi 1991) have wondered how the spiral of silence theory applies to the sudden demise of communist rule in East and Central Europe, since this does seem to be a case where a powerful and vocal minority not only effectively silenced widespread dissent, but upheld the illusion of consensus support.

The theory has been criticized for its over-pessimistic view of both human nature and of the media. Following a similar line, others have questioned its universal applicability. Moscovici (1991) suggests that we should pay less attention to silent majorities and more to 'loud minorities', who play a creative and innovative role in the life of societies. He supposes the theory to be somewhat dated, along with the traditional enlightenment notion of public opinion.

References   **Allport, G.** (1937) 'Towards a science of public opinion', *Public Opinion Quarterly*, **1**: 7–23.

Csikszentmihalyi, M. (1991) 'Reflections on the spiral of silence', pp. 288–97 in Anderson, J., (ed.), *Communication Yearbook 14*. Newbury Park, CA: Sage.

Moscovici, S. (1991) 'Silent majorities and loud minorities', pp. 298–308 in Anderson, J. (ed.), op. cit.

Noelle-Neumann, E. (1974) 'The spiral of silence: a theory of public opinion', *Journal of Communication*, **24**: 24–51.

Noelle-Neumann, E. (1984) *The spiral of silence*. Chicago: University of Chicago Press.

Noelle-Neumann, E. (1991) 'The theory of public opinion: the concept of the spiral of silence', in Anderson, J. (ed.) op. cit., pp. 256–87.

Scheff, T.J. (1967) 'Towards a sociological model of consensus', *American Sociological Review*, **32**: 32–46.

Taylor, D.G. (1982) 'Pluralistic ignorance and the spiral of silence', *Public Opinion Quarterly*, **46**: 311–55.

4.5   INFORMATION GAPS AS EFFECTS

In considering long-term effects of mass communication it is important to take into account the discussion of so-called knowledge or information gaps. A background to this discussion is formed by the steadily increasing flow of information, to a large degree made possible by mass media. This increase ought, theoretically speaking, to benefit everyone in society since every individual gets a possibility of finding their bearings in the world around them and may, perhaps, more easily enlarge their horizons. However, several researchers have lately pointed out that the increased flow of information often has the negative effect of increasing knowledge within certain groups far more than in others, and that *'information gaps'* will occur and increase, i.e. the distance between one social group and another in knowledge about a given subject.

The knowledge gap hypothesis

An early contribution in this field is the knowledge gap hypothesis of Tichenor *et al.* (1970). It claims that when the flow of information in a social system is increased, the better educated, those with a higher socio-economic status, will be able to absorb the information better than less educated people with lower status. Increased information thus results in widening the knowledge gap instead of diminishing it.

Rogers (1976) points out that information results not only in increasing *knowledge* gaps, but also in gaps concerning behaviour and attitudes. Accordingly, he changes the term to 'the communication effects gap'. He also remarks that mass communication is not the only cause of the gaps. Communication directly between individuals may also have similar effects. He finally underlines the fact that the gaps need not be caused exclusively by different levels of education – other factors may also contribute to the creation of such gaps.

Communication potential

A Swedish research group has built a discussion around the term 'communication potential' (see Nowak *et al.* 1976 and Fig. 4.5.1). The term stands for those characteristics and resources which enable the individual to give and take information, and which facilitate the communication process for him. In this discussion, the communication potential is regarded as a means of obtaining certain values in life. The size and shape of the communication potential depends on three main types of characteristics or resources:

1. Personal characteristics. We have both certain basic, often native *faculties*, like seeing and speaking, and acquired *abilities*, like speaking different languages and typewriting. Besides, we have a potential for communication, knowledge, attitudes, and traits of personality.
2. Characteristics dependent on the individual's social position. This position is defined by variables like income, education, age, and sex.
3. Characteristics of the social structure in which the individual is found. An important factor is the functioning of the individual's primary groups (e.g. family, working group), and his/her secondary groups (e.g. clubs, associations, school, organizations) when it comes to communication. In this context, society as a communication system is also relevant.

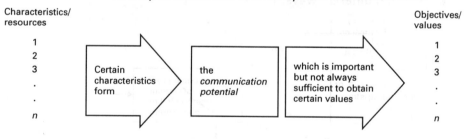

Characteristics/resources 1 2 3 . . n — Certain characteristics form — the communication potential — which is important but not always sufficient to obtain certain values — Objectives/values 1 2 3 . . n

Fig. 4.5.1 The communication potential decides whether or not an individual will attain certain values. (Nowak *et al.* 1976).

The potential may lead to the individual's obtaining certain values and reaching certain objectives. As examples of such values, the authors mention the experiencing of a sense of identity and solidarity, being able to affect one's life situation, and being able to affect society as a whole.

If we regard the above model as a model of mass media, we should consider the three types of characteristics (or resources) as independent (causal) variables. The degree of achievement of one's objectives and values then become a dependent variable (effect or consequence). In a broader perspective, we may assume the following: If, in a society, there are systematic differences between the communication potentials of different groups, this will result in systematic differences in the achievement of objectives and values of the respective groups.

From 'a gap' to 'gaps'

The phenomenon in question has been often talked about as 'the information gap' or 'the knowledge gap' in society. This is certainly an over-simplification. There exists not only one information gap, but many, and they do not look alike. It is conceivable that the information gap or knowledge gap concerning world politics is wider than that concerning the increased costs of foodstuffs during the past few years. Taking our point of departure from the various information gaps in a particular society, we would also find that the different gaps cut through the population in different ways.

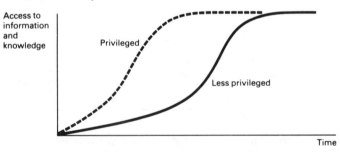

Fig. 4.5.2   Closing information gap, in which the less privileged group 'catches up' with the more privileged one (Thunberg *et al.* 1982).

It is often claimed that the gaps tend to increase as time passes.

This may be true in some cases, but Thunberg *et al.* (1979) consider that they often acquire the aspect as shown in Fig. 4.5.2. In this figure, the dotted line represents the readings-off relevant to those groups in society which are privileged in respect of communication, i.e. those with a high communication potential. The continuous line represents the corresponding development in less privileged groups. We see how the gap is at first increased, but how the less privileged category 'catches up' with the other. The final result is that the information gap is closed, as far as this particular subject goes. As an example we may consider the information campaign which preceded the change in Sweden from left-hand over to right-hand traffic. At the outset there was, to be sure, a certain information gap or knowledge gap, which later disappeared.

Some researchers term this phenomenon of the two curves approaching and joining 'ceiling effects'. Such ceilings may be reached when the potential information about the subject in question is limited. Those who have a large capacity for absorbing information after some time have no more to gather from the information flow on a particular subject. This fact enables the less privileged to catch up. It is also conceivable that a ceiling is reached when the privileged group in a certain situation no longer feels motivated for seeking more information, while the less privileged group is still motivated and in the long run becomes equally well informed (see Ettema and Kline 1977).

The American researchers Donohue *et al.* (1975) exemplify the failure of many gaps to close with reference to knowledge of space research and of the smoking and cancer issue. In both cases, the authors maintain, heavy media attention resulted in widened gaps between higher and lower educated categories. It is also conceivable that, when a subject drops out of the general discussion, so that nobody or very few talk about it any longer, the gap between privileged and underprivileged remains or may even widen. Such a development is illustrated in Fig. 4.5.3.

Comment   In a dynamic society, new information gaps appear incessantly, as various subjects increase and decrease in topicality and relevance. The conditions favourable or unfavourable to each gap vary, depending on the complexity or content of the subject. The communication potential mentioned above should, however, be a decisive factor, according to Nowak *et al.* (1976). This is especially relevant to subjects about which it is 'profitable' to be well-informed. If we are to regard the information gaps in a sociological light, the important thing is not the amount of information as such, but *what* information one is able to absorb (and transmit).

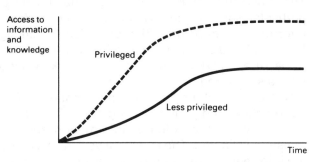

Fig. 4.5.3   Non-closing information gap (Thunberg *et al.* 1982).

The actual development of different information gaps depends on many factors. Donohue *et al.* (1975) proposed, for example, the following hypotheses which received support:

1. Where an issue arouses general concern for a community as a whole, knowledge about that issue is more likely to become more evenly distributed.
2. This equalization is more likely to occur when the issue emerges in a climate of social conflict.
3. Such equalization in knowledge is more likely to occur in a small, homogeneous community than in a large, pluralistic one.

The opinion of Rogers (1976) cited above that mass media are not the only creators of information gaps, is relevant here. In many cases, such gaps may appear because communication between individuals works better with some categories of people than with others. In one well-known American investigation, for instance, it was found that doctors who had good contact with their colleagues and frequently communicated with them, were quicker to accept new medical discoveries than doctors who were more isolated.

It is an interesting question whether different media tend to create different types of gaps. There is some evidence that television has a greater potential for closing gaps than has the press. This may be due to the fact that TV usually is a more homogeneous and limited source, whereas in the case of the press, each paper reaches different publics with a more differentiated content. Probably more significant is the fact that television is a widely trusted source and tends to reach a higher proportion of the public, in many countries, with public affairs information.

Empirical research designed to test the relationship between media and information gaps has had mixed results and produced little unequivocal evidence of an independent mass media effect. Gaziano (1983) concluded, for instance, from a review of 58 studies that, over time, 'increasing levels of media publicity may reduce gaps, but several other factors may be equally or more influential in narrowing gaps'.

New media such as various forms of televised data transmission, where information is individually consulted (see 8.3 below), may also have a tendency to widen information gaps since their use will depend on the individual's interests, motivation and previous knowledge and such media are more available to better-educated and higher-status groups.

Models of information gaps may, among other things, be seen as a reaction against a naive and exaggerated liberal belief in the ability of mass media to create a homogeneously well-informed mass of citizens. The discussion of this subject is not least important when it comes to the role of communication in the developing countries. The insights conferred by the models may decisively affect the planning of information work in such areas.

The discussion about information gaps may be seen in relation to other models and areas in mass communication research, most obviously to diffusion research, from which we have derived Rogers and Shoemaker's model in Section 3.4, and which also deals with the diffusion of news. It is also possible to relate the discussion to ideas concerning the so-called two-step flow of information hypothesis (3.2) and to the dependency model (4.3).

References Donohue, G.A., Tichenor, P.J. and Olien, C.N. (1975) 'Mass media and the knowledge gap', *Communication Research*, **2**: 3–23.

Ettema, J.S. and Kline, F.G. (1977) 'Deficits, differences and ceilings: contingent conditions for understanding the knowledge gap', *Communication Research*, **4**: 179–202.

Gaziano, C. (1983) 'The knowledge gap: an analytical review of media effects', *Communication Research*, 10, **4**: 447–86.

Nowak, K., Rosengren, K.E. and Sigurd, B. (1976) 'Kommunikation, underprivilegiering, mänskliga värden' in *Kommunikation, Social Organisation, Mänskliga Resurser*, Samarbetskommittén för Långtidsmotiverad Forskning, Stockholm.

Rogers, E.M. (1976) 'Communication and development: the passing of the dominant paradigm', *Communication Research*, **3**: 213–40.

Thunberg, A.M., Nowak, K. and Rosengren, K.E. (1982) *Communication and Equality*. Stockholm: Almquist and Wicksell.

Tichenor, P.J., Donohue, G.A. and Olien, C.N. (1970) 'Mass media and differential growth in knowledge', *Public Opinion Quarterly*, **34**: 158–70.

4.6 CENTRIFUGAL VERSUS CENTRIPETAL EFFECTS OF MEDIA IN SOCIETY

The general social effects of mass communication have, from the earliest days of social theory, been subject to quite contradictory assessments. The alternative theoretical evaluations are based not only on opposed values, but on opposing estimations of the actual consequences of the mass media. While the relevant value positions are complex and the alternative effects even more so, it is useful to summarize the main theoretical options according to two basic dimensions which summarize and capture many of the questions in dispute (Carey 1969; McQuail 1987). These two dimensions are positive versus negative valuation and centrifugal versus centripetal tendency. The first is self-explanatory; social effects are either positively valued and the media viewed optimistically or they are disliked and the media viewed with pessimism.

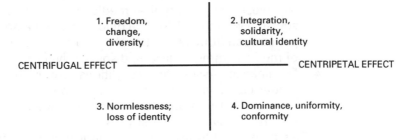

Fig. 4.6.1   Centrifugal/centripetal model: four images of societal effect from mass media.

The second dimension refers to alternative (or dual) effects from mass media. The latter can have an effect on society in the direction of dispersal and fragmention (a centrifugal effect) even though it may also be liberating. Or the media can work towards integration and unity of culture and society, strengthening social bonds and social control (the centripetal effect). The main cause of the centrifugal effect is thought to lie in the privatizing and isolating tendency of mass media – the transformation of a more local and communal form of society into a mass of disconnected individuals, who focus their attention on a dominant (often metropolitan) centre. The centripetal effect is said to derive from the spread and reinforcement of a common culture and collective consciousness by way of homogeneous central media to which all are attached (Gerbner 1972).

It is not illogical to suppose that mass media can have all the tendencies indicated, but some outcomes as depicted in Fig. 4.6.1 are more associated with certain conditions, as follows:

1. Freedom and change. This liberal vision assumes expansion and abundance of mass media channels and diversity of content, under conditions of media freedom. It represents an idealized view of what technology, liberal democracy and the free market will deliver.
2. Integration. This view is only likely to hold where national societies have strong control over their own media systems, including hardware and software and where the historical conditions for strong cultural identity are present.
3. Normlessness. The typical media and social conditions associated with this vision are of low national autonomy, high penetration from international media systems, a high degree of media commercialism and social privatization.
4. Dominance. Associated conditions are high degrees of media concentration and centralization in systems under state control or subjected to powerful media monopolies, with relatively little diversity.

This theoretical framework helps in locating and formulating some broad questions about trends in media and society, especially as a result of the increasing abundance, fragmentation and individualization of communication (see Chapter 8). For example, it has been argued that the decline in centralized national broadcasting systems may lead to a decline in national, possibly social, integration. Against this, advocates of new interactive media technologies claim that they could have an opposite, 'demassifying' and integrative effect. Which perspective one adopts depends on value preferences as well as on the facts of the case.

References   **Carey, J.** (1969) 'The communication revolution and the professional communicator', pp. 23–38 in Halmos P. (ed.), *The Sociology of Mass Media Communicators. Sociological Review Monograph, 13*. University of Keele.

Gerbner, G. (1972) 'Mass media and human communication theory', pp. 35–58 in McQuail, D., (ed.), *Sociology of Mass Communications*. Harmondsworth: Penguin.

McQuail, D. (1987) *Mass Communication Theory*, 2nd edn. London: Sage.

The audience has been central in mass communication research from the very beginning, but several of the models which have already been described point to a significant development of thinking about the audience. Initially the audience was perceived as an undifferentiated mass, as a passive target for persuasion and information, or as a market of consumers of media products. Students of media effects soon came to recognize that actual audiences are made up of real social groups and are characterized by networks of interpersonal relationships through which effects are mediated. Audiences can also resist influence, in part because they have their own varied reasons for choosing to attend to media messages. The initial mistake (following the basic one-directional model, 2.1 above) was to suppose that media choose their audiences. They aim to do so, but their selections are less decisive than the choices which audience members make of media channels and contents.

Evidence of *selective exposure* to media messages soon accumulated, showing that audiences tend to match their choice of media channels and content to their own tastes, ideas and informational needs, thus diminishing the chance of change effects from media and increasing the chances of 'reinforcement'. It was even suggested (Katz 1959) that we should pay less attention to what 'media do to people' and more to what 'people do with media'. This is the underlying premiss of the so-called 'uses and gratifications' approach, which focuses on the *uses* of media content for fulfilling needs or providing gratifications.

5.1 THE USES AND GRATIFICATIONS APPROACH

Uses and gratifications research may be divided into a 'classical' and a 'modern' period. The former includes studies carried out during the 1940s by the Bureau of Applied Social Research into New York, which led, for instance, to typologies of audience motives listening to soap operas and quiz programmes (Lazarsfeld and Stanton 1944). With these can be included Berelson's (1949) study of what readers of New York newspapers said they missed during a newspaper strike. The simple and innovatory idea was to look for the reasons for the evident appeal of media and of various types of content by asking the audience what they think, feel and appreciate on the basis of their personal media use. The approach of this early period was described by Klapper (1960) as a 'functional orientation', which could account for the appeal of 'escapist' media content. He named the simple functions of the media as: providing relaxation; stimulating the imagination; providing for 'vicarious interaction'; providing 'a common ground for social intercourse'. Variations in the motives for attending to media were also studied as variables in effect research (Blumler and McQuail 1968).

5.1.1 The basic formula

An important step in the emergence of a 'modern' phase in uses and gratifications research was the escape from the shadow of *effect* research. The audience came, during the 1960s and early 1970s, to be studied in its own right, with its choices and responses to media as requiring understanding and explanation independently of any consideration of media effect. A key event in the emergence of a new school of theory and research was the publication of a collection of articles under the title *The Uses of Mass Communication* (Blumler and Katz 1974). This volume provided a description of the underlying logic of investigations into media uses and the gratifications derived from them as follows: 'They are concerned with (1) the social and psychological origins of (2) needs, which generate (3) expectations of (4) the mass media and other sources, which lead to (5) differential patterns of media exposure (or engagement in other activities), resulting in (7) other consequences, perhaps mostly unintended ones.' This statement is expressed in model form in Fig. 5.1.1.

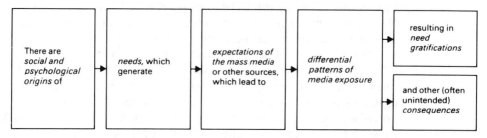

Fig. 5.1.1   The elements of a uses and gratifications model.

This model involves certain assumptions about the audience, but especially that the audience is *active* and makes motivated choices, based on previous experience with the media. There is also an assumption that media use is only one way amongst others of satisying needs which are experienced in everyday life. For instance, with reference to the needs relating to social inter-action or intercourse mentioned above, we can suppose that media are looked to in order to provide either acceptable alterna-tives to real human companionship or the basis for making con-tact with others (talking about media content or information gained from media). Of course, there are more direct ways of enjoying social interaction, although they may not be readily available (Rosengren and Windahl 1972).

5.1.2   Rosengren's general model

A further elaboration of the basic thinking described above was provided by Rosengren (1974) in the form of a model reproduced in Fig. 5.1.2.

The 'needs' of the individual form the starting point (1) (reference is made to Maslow's (1954) hierarchy of human needs), but for these to lead to relevant action they have to be perceived as problems (4) and some potential solution has also to be perceived (5). In the model, the experience of needs is shown to be shaped or influenced by (3) aspects of the social structure (level of development, type of political system) and also by (2) individual characteristics (e.g. personality, social or life-cycle position). The perception of problems and possible solutions leads to the formulation of motives (6) for media use (7) or other kinds of behaviour (8).

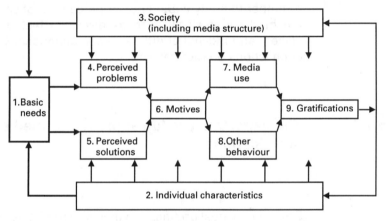

Fig. 5.1.2   Paradigm for uses and gratifications research (Rosengren 1974).

According to Rosengren, 'motives are difficult to distinguish empirically from needs and problems, but analytically they are different'. For the most part, the motives so indicated are the same as the gratifications (sought or expected) which much research has tried to identify and to bring together within a framework or typology. An example of the latter is to be found in McQuail *et al.*'s (1972) typology of 'media–person interactions' consisting of four main items: 'Diversion'; 'Personal relationships'; 'Personal identity'; 'Surveillance'. Media use in the model refers primarily to selecting and paying attention by reading, listening, viewing, etc. (differential media consumption). According to the theory of uses and gratifications, content will be selected and used in ways which help in the solution of perceived problems. Alternative (to media use) behaviour (8) could also provide a solution, possibly even more directly and naturally, as when a need for social contact is satisfied by going to visit friends – (see Rosengren and Windahl 1972).

The last step in the journey portrayed in the model is the experience (or not) of satisfaction of the needs which existed at the outset. The connecting lines back to social structure (2) and individual differences (3) are intended to cover the theoretical possibility that motivated media use could have some independent effects on individuals and society. The connection is also a reminder that any experience or perception of satisfaction from the media is itself likely to be directly affected or shaped by society and individual differences, independently of any causal connections on motives and use.

5.1.3   The expectancy-value approach to media gratifications

Essential to most gratification theory of media use is the idea that media use offers rewards which can be expected (thus predicted) by members of the audience, on the basis of past experience with the media. These rewards can be considered as psychological effects which are valued by individuals. Palmgreen and Rayburn (1985) have reformulated uses and gratifications theory as having centrally to do with an increment of valued satisfactions obtained relative to an original expectation. They want to clarify the meaning of the concept 'expectations' and they do so by distinguishing an *empirical* from an *evaluative* aspect, following work on the study of attitudes by Fishbein and Ajzen (1975). People behave on the basis of a perceived probability that an action will have a particular consequence and they also value that outcome in varying degrees. However, these two elements are conceptually and analytically distinct. They also see these ideas as providing a way of explaining media use behaviour, as shown in Fig. 5.1.3.

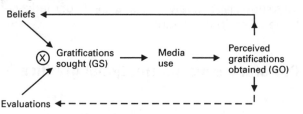

Fig. 5.1.3 An expectancy-value model of media gratifications sought and obtained (Palmgreen and Rayburn 1985).

The elements in the model are formally related as follows:

$$GS_i = b_i e_i$$

where GS_i = the $_i$th gratification sought from some media object X (medium, programme or content type); b_i = the belief (subjective probability) that X possesses some attribute or that a behaviour related to X will have a particular outcome; and e_i = the affective evaluation of the particular attribute or outcome.

In general, this model expresses the proposition that media use is accounted for by a combination of perception of benefits offered by the medium and the differential valuation of these perceived benefits. This helps to take care of the fact that media use is shaped by *avoidance* as well as by positive choice, and also by the varying degrees of positive gratifications which are expected. It also clearly distinguishes, analytically at least, the time dimension, thus the matter of when gratifications are measured. Early research tended to make no distinction between past recollection of gratifications obtained and future hopes of gratifications.

The model formally identifies a potential *increment* over time from media use behaviour. For instance, where 'Gratifications obtained' is noticeably greater than 'Gratifications expected' (or sought) then we identify situations of high audience satisfaction and expect to find high ratings of appreciation and attention. The reverse pattern can also occur, providing clues to rising or falling audience ratings. One of the main implications for research noted by the authors of this model is that it requires investigators to explore a greater range of media attributes along both the belief and the evaluation dimensions than has generally been the case up to now. Negatively valued aspects of media content have also to be taken into account.

5.1.4   Cultural versus informational gratification models

In line with the distinction made earlier between a 'ritual' and an 'instrumental' model (see 2.7), it has been suggested (McQuail 1984) that it is inappropriate to deploy the same thinking and the same audience 'uses and gratifications' model for all kinds of mass media content and use. The mainstream approach is essentially utilitarian in its thinking, assuming a logical relationship between means (media use) and ends (gratifications) which can be charted and measured. It mirrors the main features of the 'transmission model' described earlier (2.7). This may fit much informational media use, but does not seem to match the more frequently occurring circumstances of recreational and imaginative use of media, which may for convenience be described as 'cultural' rather than 'informational'.

Moreover, it has been observed that much use of media is undertaken *in order to* escape from reality (see Katz and Foulkes 1962), to be 'carried away' or to be 'lost' or 'caught up' in a world of the imagination. There are a wide range of phenomena involved, but general features are high levels of 'arousal', 'involvement' and affective engagement. According to McQuail (1984), 'the essence of this general sensation is to free the spectator . . . mentally from the immediate constraints and/or dullness of daily life and to enable him or her to enter into new experiences vicariously which would would not otherwise be available (except by use of the imagination)'. The relevant point here is that such a process cannot easily be mapped on the audience use models described above, since it tends towards detachment of audience members from 'reality' rather than connecting them more effectively with it.

For this reason a quite different kind of model is required for what can be termed 'cultural' experience with media, especially attention paid to affective/imaginative content and, generally, uses of media which follow a more 'ritual', consummatory, pattern than an instrumental one. A 'culturalist' model of media use has to recognize two meanings of culture – one the set of cultural texts, products and practice which comprise the media experience (and the 'media culture'), another the different tastes and preferences which guide individual choice amongst what the media make available. Cultural taste, in this sense, refers to an individual attribute (the particular preference pattern) which is shaped by family, social class milieu, education and generally the 'cultural capital' available to an individual (Bourdieu 1986). In the simplest terms, personal cultural taste guides media content preferences and choices (for particular genres, formats, types of content) and leads to various kinds of affective and emotional satisfactions. One result of the operation of systematic selection based on tastes is the development of 'taste cultures', referring to organized sets of cultural artefacts which are not united by any clear aesthetic or by the preference of a class or social group. The model in Fig. 5.1.4 shows the relationship between the elements described.

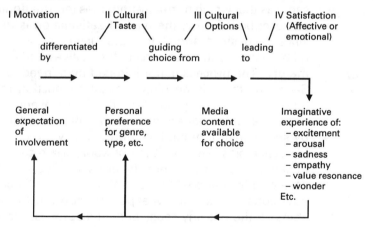

Fig. 5.1.4   A model of 'cultural' media use (McQuail 1984).

As with the 'dominant' uses model, there is an implied sequence, since the general inclination to seek cultural experience *precedes* actual involvement, as does the pattern or 'set' of cultural taste, which is shaped by social context as well as personality. The cultural options are also largely 'given' in advance, although often varied. In the model, choice and attention are assumed to be generally purposeful (looking for involvement, escape, diversion, emotional release, etc.) but may often be unspecific. Attention to media content is followed by reflection on the experience, with potential consequences for subsequent cultural choices and for reinforcing (or undermining) the personal taste pattern. This is reflected by the return 'loop' from experience to sense of 'involvement' and to personal cultural taste.

If this model is compared to an equivalent 'informational' (and more instrumental) model, we would recognize as Step I a general factor of interest, curiosity or 'need to know'. The equivalent of 'cultural taste' is a set of topic or field 'interests'. These are also shaped by social background, as is the 'accessibility' of the available information options. There are subsequent informational or social satisfactions to inventorize under headings such as 'surveillance', 'application of knowledge', 'advice', 'social exchange', etc.

Nevertheless, the process represented in Fig. 5.1.4 is not the same as that which normally underlies informational media uses as described. Firstly, the type of satisfaction is quite different, since the desired 'end-states' (gratifications sought) are not useful or instrumental, but ends in themselves and purely consummatory. The process is not initiated by a 'need' or a 'problem'. Secondly, there is no direct causal connection to be imputed between social background and the nature of any cultural experience, even if the pattern of taste may be shaped in some degree by social environment. It is more directly the result of personal idiosyncrasies. Thirdly, it is not appropriate to account for the observed media behaviours in terms of 'effects', as we can in the case of informational and social uses of media content (which have consequences for what people know and for social relationships). If there is any cause and effect process, according to the cultural model, the experience with media culture can only be considered as an outcome, not a cause. More likely it is neither; simply a moment in time.

Comment   The uses and gratifications approach was designed originally to help account for the appeal of different kinds of media and to help in the explanation and prediction of differences in media effect. It has some limited success in this respect (Blumler and McQuail 1968; Rosengren and Windahl 1989), but its main contribution has been towards a better description of the audience, of audience behaviour and of different media and different kinds or examples of content in terms of their audience appeal. It has received a good deal of criticism over the years, some of it on rather scholastic grounds – it was said to be too functionalistic, psychologistic and individualistic, lending itself to the manipulative purpose of the media managers and insensitive to social structural determination (Elliott 1974). Some more specific limitations which have been noted include the following:

1. It overemphasizes the 'activity' of the audience, in the face of evidence showing that much television at least is viewed with little selectivity (Barwise and Ehrenberg 1988).
2. It is rather insensitive to media content itself, largely ignoring the textual and cultural specifics of media content.

Some of the points of critique have been addressed in more recent work but the alternative approaches to the audience described in 5.2 and 5.3 suggest that we may need to choose a completely different set of assumptions and a quite different approach if we are dissatisfied with this particular tradition.

References   Barwise, D. and Ehrenberg, A. (1988) *Television and its Audience*. London: Sage.

Berelson, B. (1949) 'What missing the newspaper means' in Lazarsfeld, P.F. and Stanton, F. (eds) *Radio Research 1948–9*. New York: Harper and Row.

Blumler, J.G. and Katz, E. (eds) (1974) *The Uses of Mass Communications*. Beverly Hills, CA: Sage.

Blumler, J.G. and McQuail, D. (1968) *Television in Politics: its Uses and Influence*. London: Faber and Faber.

Bourdieu, P. (1986) *Distinction: a Social Critique of the Judgement of Taste*. London: Routledge.

Elliott, P. (1974) 'Uses and gratifications research: a critique of a sociological perspective' in Blumler, J.G. and Katz, E. (eds), op. cit.

Fishbein, M. and Ajzen, I. (1975) *Belief, Attitude, Intention and Behavior*. Reading, MA: Addison-Wesley.

Katz, E. (1959) 'Mass communication research and the study of culture', *Studies in Public Communication*, **2**: 1–16.

Katz, E. and **Foulkes, D.** (1962) 'On the use of mass media as "escape"', *Public Opinion Quarterly* **26**: 377–88

Katz, E., Blumler J.G. and **Gurevitch, M.** (1974) 'Utilization of mass communication by the individual', pp. 19–32 in Blumler, J.G. and Katz, E. (eds) op. cit.

Klapper, J. (1960) *The Effects of Mass Communication.* New York: Free Press.

Lazarsfeld, P.F. and **Stanton, F.** (1944) (eds) *Radio Research 1942–3.* New York: Duell, Sloan and Pearce.

McQuail, D. (1984) 'With the benefit of hindsight: reflections on uses and gratifications research', *Critical Studies in Mass Communication*, 1, **2**: 177–93.

McQuail, D., Blumler, J.G. and **Brown, J.** (1972) 'The television audience: a revised perspective', pp. 135–65 in McQuail, D. (ed.) *Sociology of Mass Communications.* Harmondsworth: Penguin.

Maslow, A.H. (1954) *Motivation and Personality.* New York: Harper and Brothers.

Palmgreen, P. and **Rayburn, J.D.** (1985) 'An expectancy-value approach to media gratifications', pp. 61–73 in Rosengren, J.E., Palmgreen, P. and Wenner, L. (eds) *Media Gratification Research.* Beverly Hills and London: Sage.

Rosengren, K.E. (1974) 'Uses and gratifications: a paradigm outlined' pp. 269–81 in Blumler, J.G., and Katz, E (eds) *The Uses of Mass Communications.*

Rosengren, K.E. and **Windahl, S.** (1972) 'Mass media consumption as a functional alternative', pp. 166–94 in McQuail, D. (ed.) *Sociology of Mass Communications.* Harmondsworth: Penguin.

Rosengren, K.E. and **Windahl, S.** (1989) *Media Matter.* Norwood, NJ: Ablex.

5.2 RENCKSTORF'S SOCIAL ACTION MODEL

The main theoretical thrust of Renckstorf's (1989) revision of the uses and gratifications approach is based on a wish to place the audience as central and dominant in the mass communication process. Essential points, drawn from symbolic interactionism and phenomenology in particular, include the following. People

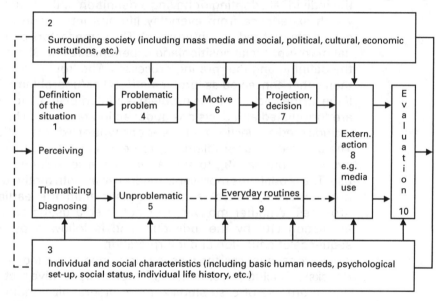

Fig. 5.2.1   Social action model of media use (Renckstorf 1989).

engage in activity on the basis of their own objectives, intentions and interests, but they are in interaction with many others and are capable of reflecting on their own actions and interactions. Human beings are not determined, but can reflect on their 'life-world' which they share with others. Individuals have to interpret their situation and act accordingly. In the normal way of things, everyday life is 'unproblematic', since recurring problems are provided with solutions. The media are also not to be considered as 'stimuli' which provoke a reaction from audiences and they form only part of the relevant 'meaning producing symbolic environment' of human actors. The individual has a self-image and engages in an interaction with self in which media can become involved.

This perspective has led to a revision of the earlier models presented, on the lines shown in Fig. 5.2.1. The basic framework of an interactive and recurrent process suggested by Rosengren (see Fig. 5.1.2) remains the same, but the starting point is different and alternative options are presented. At the outset (1) we see the individual adopting or having a definition of the situation, in which experience from everyday life and interaction are perceived, thematized and interpreted. The same factors of individual make-up, social position and experience (2 and 3) enter into the defining and interpreting processes. The 'route' followed is then either conceived as 'problematic' (4) or 'unproblematic' (5). If the former, action on the problem is contemplated, motives (6) are formulated and decisions about action taken (7). These can include media selection and use as one type of external action (8). The alternative, unproblematic, route can also lead, by way of everyday routines (9), to similar actions, also including media use. The model thus represents media use as both motivated and not motivated, which is more realistic than the earlier approaches. Whether motivated or not, media use is subject to evaluation (10) by the individual and is followed by a new sequence of definition and interpretation.

The consequences for research into media use indicated by Renckstorf include an enhanced role for interpretative methodology, more use of case studies, more biographical inquiry and more qualitative approaches in general.

References   **Renckstorf, K.** (1989) 'Medienutzung als soziales Handeln', in *Kölner Zeitschrift für Soziologie und Sozialpsychologie*, Sonderheft, **30**: 314–36.

Renckstorf, K. and **Wester, F.** (1992) 'Die handlungstheoretische perspektive empirischer (massen-) kommunikationsforschung', in *Communications*, **17**, 2: 177-92.

5.3   AUDIENCE RECEPTION AND DECODING

An alternative approach to the study of audience experience can be identified under the broad heading of 'reception analysis'. This has its origins in traditions of media study which differ from those underlying the uses and gratifications approach. In particular, it has developed out of critical theory, semiology and discourse analysis and also from ethnographic studies of media use. It is located more in the domain of the cultural than of the social sciences. According to Jensen and Rosengren (1990), reception analysis questions the predominant methodologies of empirical social-scientific research and also the humanistic studies of content because both are unable or unwilling to take account of the 'power of the audience' in giving meaning to messages.

The essence of the 'reception approach' is to locate the attribution and construction of meaning (derived from media) with the receiver. Media messages are always 'polysemic' (having multiple meanings) and have to be interpreted. According to Jensen (1991) 'mass media reception . . . is an integrated aspect of the everyday practices of communities and specific cultural groups and should be studied in its social and discursive content'. Some elements of this view are included in Renckstorf's model (5.2), but reception analysis emphasizes the existence of discrete 'interpretative communities' which are much more paramount and autonomous than the uses and gratifications approach allows.

Jensen and Rosengren (1990) characterize the essence of the approach as follows:

Drawing on methods of analysis-cum-interpretation from the literary tradition and the conception of communication and cultural processes as socially situated discourse from cultural studies, reception analysis can be said to perform a comparative reading of media discourses and audience discourses in order to understand the processes of reception.

The main differences from the uses and gratifications approach, in line with this, are: greater message-centrality; disregard of the social system; preference for ethnographic, interpretative and qualitative methodology; lack of any causal reasoning.

5.3.1   A model of encoding and decoding

Amongst the forerunners of reception analysis was an eloquent variant of critical theory formulated by Stuart Hall (1980) which emphasized the stages of transformation through which any media message passes on the way from its origins to its reception and interpretation. The main elements are presented in Fig. 5.3.1.

The theory was formulated in relation to television but could apply to any mass medium. It drew from, but also challenged, the basic principles of structuralism and semiology which presumed that any meaningful 'message' is constructed from signs which can have denotative and connotative meanings, depending on the choices made by an 'encoder'. Even so, the main thrust of semiology is that the range of meaning depends very much on the nature of the language and on the significance attaching to the patterned arrangement of given signs and symbols within a culture shared by sender (encoder) and receiver (decoder) alike. Semiology emphasizes the power of the encoded text and sees the location of meaning as firmly embedded in it. Hall accepted some elements of this approach but challenged the basic assumption, on two grounds. Firstly, communicators choose to encode messages for ideological purposes and manipulate language and media for those ends (media messages are given a 'preferred reading', or what is now called 'spin'). Secondly, receivers are not obliged to accept or decode messages as sent but can and do resist ideological influence by applying variant or oppositional readings, according to their own experience and outlook.

The path followed through the stages of the model is simple in principle. Communication originates within media institutions which constitute typical and recurrent frameworks of meaning, likely to conform to dominant power structures. Specific messages are 'encoded', often in the form of established content genres (such as 'news', 'pop music', 'sport reports', 'soap operas', 'police/detective series') which have a face-value meaning and inbuilt guidelines for interpretation by an audience. The highly complex culture of a medium such as television encompasses a wide range of discourses. The contents offered by media are approached by their audiences in terms of other 'meaning structures', which have their origin in the ideas and experience of individuals.

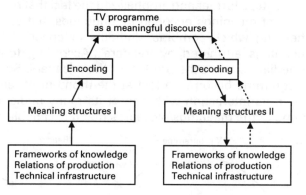

Fig. 5.3.1   Hall's encoding/decoding model (Hall 1980).

Often different groups of people (or sub-cultures) will share quite distinct social locations and perceive the world and the messages of the media accordingly. While the general implication is that meaning as decoded does not necessarily (or often) correspond with meaning as encoded (despite the mediation of conventional genres and shared language systems), the most significant point is that decoding can take a quite different course from that intended. Receivers can read between the lines and even reverse and 'subvert' the intended direction of the message (indicated by broken arrow lines in 5.3.1).

It is clear that this model and the associated theory embodies several of the principles stated above: the multiplicity of meanings; the existence of 'interpretative' communities; the primacy of the receiver in determining meaning. At the time when this approach was formulated, it was left to the skilled cultural analyst to determine the range and distribution of possible interpretations. Reception analysis has been developed partly in order to give a role and a voice to the 'receivers' to speak for themselves (e.g. Morley 1980).

5.3.2   A discourse model

More recent developments of the same line of thinking have gone
some steps further and emphasized the fact that media 'texts' are
not just meanings encoded in languages, but constructions of
meaning which combine elements of encoded text with the
meanings attributed by 'readers'. According to Fiske (1987),
'[media] texts are the product of their readers. So a [television]
programme becomes a text at the moment of reading, that is,
when its interaction with one of its many audiences activates
some of the meanings/pleasures that it is capable of provoking'

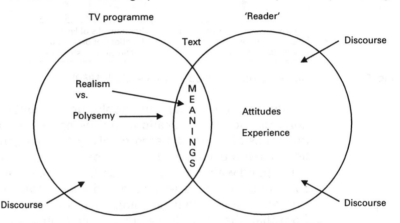

Fig. 5.3.2   A media discourse model (based on theory in Fiske 1987).

(p.14). He further introduces the concept of 'discourse' as essential to studying the process of text production. A discourse is
defined as 'a language or system of representation that has
developed socially in order to make and circulate a coherent set
of meanings about an important topic area'. The idea of discourse so defined corresponds quite closely to the idea of 'meaning structure' as used by Hall (1980). In Fiske's presentation, the
multiplicity of meanings (polysemy) of media texts is not only a
demonstrated fact but essential to media if they are to be popular
with a wide range of different sorts of people, in different social

situations, who bring their divergent frameworks of meaning to bear on the same media content. These ideas are captured in Fig. 5.3.2.

The main point illustrated is that a meaningful text is located in the overlap/correspondence between the discursive world of an audience and the discourse embodied in the media text. Contributing to the meaning established are the experiences and orientations of the 'reader' (in this case television viewer). On the side of the TV programme discourse, an important variable will be the degree of realism or polysemy. The more 'realistic' the programme, the more constrained are the meanings which can be established or shared with an audience of readers; the more 'polysemic', and thus content which is 'open' in form and relatively lacking in 'preferred' meanings, the more scope for varied texts to be produced and alternative meanings taken from the same message. While this discussion appears to relate to the content and possible *effect* of messages, in fact the reception analysis approach does not distinguish between the 'meanings' of a text and the 'pleasures' or satisfactions experienced. The latter have to be as much constructed by the receiver as the 'message' or supposed 'content'.

Comment   The research which has been opened up by this perspective is diverse in kind, but there have been three main kinds of yield so far.

- One area of research is into the experience of particular groups of readers or 'fans', an example being the study by Radway (1984) of women readers of romances.
- A second is the research attention to the immediate family or domestic context of media use, applying ethnographic methods (e.g. Silverstone 1991; Lull 1988; Morley 1986).
- A third is represented by the numerous studies into the differential cross-cultural reception of the same popular programme content (for instance, the series Dallas) (Liebes and Katz 1986). This work was pioneered by enquiries into differential reception of news (Morley 1980).

The reception analysis approach leads to qualitatively rich findings, but as Jensen and Rosengren (1990) point out, 'its

findings are not easily replicable' and can rarely be general-
ized beyond the small groups of individuals which are typically studied. They also tend to see the approach as
complementary to 'uses and gratifications' research, rather
than as an alternative. While reception analysis is not obviously either 'socially relevant' or much use to practitioners, it
does contribute to the 'empowerment' of audiences – recog-
nizing the autonomous role of the receiver in the attainment
of any response or effect and the potential for resisting
manipulation by way of 'subversive' or alternative readings.
In a multi-channel and -choice environment, media providers
also have a greater need to have a more rounded and deeper
knowledge of their multiple 'target audiences' and can depend less on the ratings which are the staple ingredient of
traditional audience and media market research.

References   **Ang, I.** (1989) Syllabus 'Introduction to Mass Communication'. Department of
Communication, University of Amsterdam.
Fiske, J. (1987) *Television Culture*. London: Routledge.
Hall, S. (1980) 'Encoding, decoding in the television discourse' in Hall, S., Hobson,
D. and Lowe, P., (eds) *Culture, Media, Language*. London: Hutchinson.
Jensen, K.B. (1991) 'When is meaning? Communication theory, pragmatism and
mass media reception', pp. 3–32 in Anderson, J.A. (ed.), *Communication Year-
book, 14*. Newbury Park, CA: Sage.
Jensen, K.B. and **Rosengren, K.E.** (1990) 'Five traditions in search of the audience',
European Journal of Communication, 5, **2–3**: 207–38.
Liebes, T. and **Katz, E.** (1986) 'Patterns of involvement in television fiction': a
comparative analysis'. *European Journal of Communication*, 2, **3**: 151–72.
Lull, J. (ed.), (1988) *World Families Watch Television*. Newbury Park, CA: Sage.
Morley, J. (1980) 'The "nationwide" audience: structure and decoding'. *Televi-
sion Monographs, 11*. London: British Film Institute.
Morley, J. (1986) *Family Television*. London: Comedia.
Radway, J. (1984) *Reading the Romance*. Chapel Hill, NC: University of North
Carolina Press.
Silverstone, R. (1991) 'From audiences to consumers: the household and the
consumption of communication and information technologies', *European
Journal of Communication*, 6, **2**: 135–54.

5.4 AUDIENCE REACH, CHOICE AND APPRECIATION

A feature of mass communication which from the beginning stimulated research was the 'invisibility' of the audience. Those who operated or used the media had an urgent need to know the who, when and how many of their unseen public. This was especially true of radio and television broadcasting where, without research, the size of audience can only be very indirectly and crudely estimated. By contrast, music, books, magazines, films and newspapers all yield some direct evidence of audience attention and interest. In the case of broadcasting, not only is the size of the audience unknown, but the quality of reception is extremely unpredictable, with very variable attention and much switching between channels.

Broadcasters are largely dependent on research (after the event) to know three basic facts about their audience: its size for different channels and programmes; the degree of attention given; and the degree of satisfaction or appreciation. Uncertainty has generated much ingenuity in attempts to overcome the problems which arise. The increase in the number of channels made possible by new technologies and (especially by cable and satellite) international transmission has exacerbated the situation, making the 'audience' even less predictable and unstable.

5.4.1 A model of differential audience reach

The essential features of the audience as seen from the point of view of the would-be communicator are captured in Fig. 5.4.1, taken from the work of the Belgian researcher, Roger Clausse (1968).

Although this model can apply, in principle, to all mass media it was developed for the case of broadcasting. The outer band represents the almost unlimited potential for the reception of broadcast messages. The second band indicates the realistic

maximum limits which apply to reception – delineating the
potential media public, which is defined by residence in geo-
graphical areas of reception and by possession of the necessary

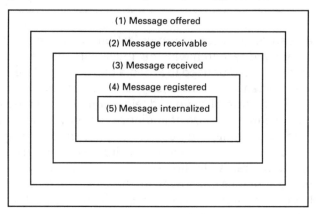

Fig. 5.4.1   A schema of differential audience reach (Clausse 1968).

apparatus to receive. This potential audience is not fixed, but can
vary according to the ease of individual access to receiving equipment and by the availability of recording and play-back equipment. It also depends on a particular definition of availability or
eligibility. For instance, the potential audience might exclude
children under a certain age and certain other categories of viewers or listeners. For some purposes the 'potential audience' has
also to take account of time of day – distinguishing, for instance,
between an early-morning, a day-time and an evening audience.

The third band identifies another level of media public – the
actual audience reached by a radio or television channel or programme. This is what is usually measured by *audience ratings*
(often expressed as a percentage of the potential audience). The
fourth band and centre refer to degrees of attention, impact and
effect, some of which are empirically measurable according to
ability to recognize and recall content and by the amount of time
spent with a given programme. In his discussion, Clausse comments on the extraordinary degree of instability of audiences and
also on the 'wastage' represented by this diagram, since most
broadcast messages only receive a minute degree of their potential attention and impact. He also draws attention to the qual-

itative differences between media publics, which range from a condition of 'communion' where scattered individuals may be brought together by the medium in an intense and shared experience by certain kinds of broadcast, through one of coherent togetherness, to a mass condition (conglomeration of individuals), represented by the varied, casual, habitual use of the media for unplanned diversion.

5.4.2 Television programme choice

Most media industry practitioners join with theorists of media 'uses and gratifications' in assuming that the audience has certain tastes, interests and preferences which will be consistently related to the choice of particular types of content. For the media industry it is important in policy and planning to have some idea what the preferences of the audience are likely to be. Unfortunately, the assumption of audience consistency and logic has not found much empirical support, mainly because television (and radio) use is a very habitual and unthinking activity, in which the satisfactions offered by the medium as such (e.g., just watching television) tend to swamp the particular programme or content-based motivations and choices (Barwise and Ehrenberg 1988). With this in mind, Webster and Wakshlag (1983) constructed a model of programme choice, which tries to arrange the main explanatory factors relating to programme choice in a systematic way, but giving relatively more weight to non-content factors in the viewing situation. Their model makes three assumptions: one that the structure of available programme options is fixed; second, that television is a 'free good', so that simultaneously available programmes have the same cost to the viewer; third the model is specific to an individual viewer at a single point in time (although choices are open to aggregation).

The primary *dependent variable* (the main factor to be explained) is *programme choice*. The general drift of the explanatory model can be described as follows, with numbers identifying

the relevant arrows in Fig. 5.4.2. Choice of a specific programme
for viewing at a given moment is governed, first of all, by a viewer
being available to view (1) and, secondly, by the programmes
which are on offer at that point in time (2). The actual viewing

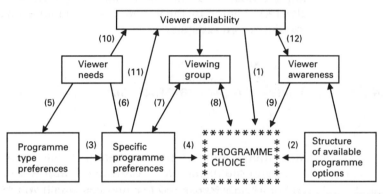

 Fig. 5.4.2   A model of television programme choice (Webster and Wakshlag 1983).

choice is normally made from a category of programmes which
the viewer generally likes (programme type preference) (3). It is
possible that the actual choice is not the same as a specific
programme of the same type which the individual would really
prefer to view (for instance a different news broadcast on another
channel) (4). A general background variable which accounts for
programme *preferences* (5 and 6) (but not actual choice) is the
factor of 'viewer needs' which refers to the motives, interests and
expectations discussed above (5.1). The two other specific determining factors in relation to choice are: the influence of a *viewing
group* (e.g. family circle), in which choices may have to be made
collectively or consensually (7 and 8); the *awareness* by a viewer
that a programme of a preferred kind is available (9).

The pathways of influence are shown by directional arrows.
Some of the arrows flow back *towards* the viewer, some are
two-directional. In particular, we can note that viewer availability
is influenced by longer-term 'needs' (10), by established preferences for certain content (11) and, more immediately, by awareness of what is available (12). Some of the separate elements in
the model can be briefly explained as follows:

Structure of programme options: At a given point in time, the number of options is no more than the number of channels in a system at a point in time (sometimes referred to as the 'horizontal' dimension of choice). Real choice is often restricted by competing schedulers offering the same type of programme at the same time. Where a viewer has an established *loyalty* to a particular channel, choice may be further constrained. Aside from limiting actual choice, the programme schedule has a marked effect on choice through the 'inheritance effect', the tendency for a viewer to stay watching the same channel which is already tuned in.

Programme type preference: While it is often assumed that viewers have consistent preferences for certain kinds of content, it has been very difficult to establish whether many viewers actually deploy a commonly held set of programme categories. Webster and Wakshlag think it is a research priority to identify the shape of any such category system.

Viewer availability: This can be conceptualized in a variety of ways and, especially, in more or less active terms. In a passive version, 'availability' can refer to having a television set and some time for viewing. Actively conceived, it implies a conscious search for some media experience to satisfy needs. As Webster and Wakshlag remark, 'availability infuses choice behaviour with considerable variation that has nothing to do with specific television content' and it is the 'single factor which is most responsible for the absence of content-based patterns of viewing'.

Viewing group: Theories of audience selection often ignore the fact that television viewing usually occurs in the company of friends and family. This fact alone could explain much of the seeming randomness of individual programme choice (e.g., the lack of consistency in viewing succeeding episodes of series – Barwise and Ehrenberg 1988). As the model indicates, the (composition of) viewing group itself may also be influenced by the progamme choice as well as vice versa.

Awareness: There are many degrees of awareness of the programme options available. Awareness refers not only to knowledge of what is in the schedule, but also to *attitudes* of like or dislike towards content which are strong enough to influence choice (see 5.1.3). Lack of awareness, in either sense, is likely to contribute to the randomness of audience behaviour which has been mentioned.

5.4.3   Audience choice under conditions of channel abundance

Much of the thinking about television audience choice referred to in this chapter has related to conditions in which audience members were faced with a limited number of rather similar channels. Increasingly, with the spread of cable, these conditions do not hold. According to Heeter (1988), for instance, cable television changes the media environment in three main ways. Firstly, the sheer number of channels makes awareness of alternatives more and more difficult for viewers and makes the task of selection much more complex. Secondly, a number of specialist channels have appeared (e.g., news, films, sport, music) which makes it easier to link preference to actual viewing. Thirdly, remote-control selectors facilitate channel changing and more active use of TV sets.

To cope with the changed conditions, Heeter proposes a new information-processing model of programme choice which takes into account whether and how viewers make themselves aware of programme alternatives. Essentially, the model proposes that viewers develop a strategy for selection, guided by programme information and observation, that they employ on a regular basis. The main new elements in the model are concepts of 'channel familiarity' and 'channel repertoire' (the set of channels watched regularly by an individual or household). The main processes involved are: use of programme guides for information; orientating searches to see what is available; decision to view; periodic re-evaluation of viewing choice. The general sequence is likely to be: informed search, with particular reference to an already established 'repertoire' of channels; decision to view; re-evaluation; renewed search, etc. Initial empirical testing of the model validated the main concepts and processes but also indicated that the information-processing skills involved are very unevenly distributed in the population.

This model tends to reassert the significance of content factors and the probability of more informed and active choices, less determined by the chance of what happens to be available. These features are also likely to be accentuated by the spread of individual receiver ownership and videorecorders.

5.4.4   Television programme appreciation

A question lying beyond viewer selection (and the ratings which derive from the sum of individual choices), is that of audience response, evaluation or appreciation. The measurement of 'quality' of reception (as distinct from the quantitative ratings of television) has provoked much debate. It is often pointed out that the intrinsic quality of a programme cannot simply be assessed by percentage viewing figures. Aside from arguments about the relationship between quality and popularity, it is clear from 5.4.2 that many factors which have nothing to do with any merits of content play a large part in determining choice (e.g., timing, group viewing, alternatives available). One of the main obstacles to measuring perceptions of 'quality' is the uncertainty over what this means. Often, it simply refers to a high degree of audience satisfaction (liking), but sometimes it refers to an attribution (by viewers or others) of intrinsic merit to content, presentation, acting, etc., independently of actual *enjoyment*.

It is also evident from audience research experience that 'quantity' and 'quality' ratings are not very closely correlated (Leggatt 1991). This is partly a result of the low degree of audience selectivity, but it is also because viewers can and do make distinctions between what they admire and what they actually choose to watch. There is a good deal of disagreement over methods for measuring quality and it is not always clear what can be done with the results when they are obtained. Nevertheless, indicators of *audience appreciation* of programmes (independently of the 'ratings') can be important for broadcasters personally and for policy and decision-making.

The model in Fig. 5.4.3 distinguishes between those factors (shown on the left) which can be considered as 'viewer' side variables and those (on the right) which are content/presentation (medium) variables.

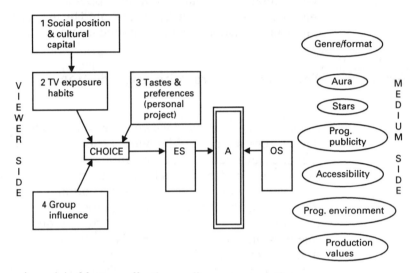

Fig. 5.4.3   A model of factors affecting audience appreciation.

The main variable to be explained is the level of audience appreciation (A) received by a programme. Most of the potential explanatory variables on the 'viewer' side are the same as those which apply to selection in Fig. 5.4.2. As depicted, each choice is accompanied by an expectation of some satisfaction (ES) (more or less the same as 'Gratifications sought' in Fig. 5.1.3), against which the actually obtained satisfaction (OS) is mentally tested by the individual viewer. A positive balance (OS > ES) is likely to produce high appreciation ratings and vice versa. In other words, audience appreciation (A) in this model is an empirical outcome of matching experience with expectation. It is not the same as judgement of intrinsic quality. The main factors on the content side which are likely to contribute to the level of satisfaction are as follows:

- **Genre or format**, which refers to a genre preference against which an actual programme experience may be matched.
- **Aura**, referring to some artistic or cultural value attaching to

certain content examples and which a viewer recognizes and appreciates.

- **Stars**: a programme with celebrity appeal is more likely to gain high appreciation as a result of their presence.
- **Publicity**: advance publicity can generate expectations of quality which are either fulfilled or not; it may even be persuasive of quality independently of experience.
- **Accessibility** refers mainly to the level of difficulty or familiarity for viewers. Inability to recognize artistic or intellectual qualities can lead to low appreciation ratings.
- **Programme environment** refers to the comparisons with other programmes available around the time or on other channels, which affect *relative* levels of appreciation.
- **Production values.** As with 'stars', content may be judged according to expectations concerning sets, location shooting, costumes, music, actuality, movement, etc.

The predominant test of satisfaction obtained may be the self-perceived degree of *involvement* achieved by individual audience members in the case of fictional/imaginative content or of *learning* in the case of informational content (see 5.1.4). As noted above, audience appreciation as treated in this model should not be confused with audience attributions of programme intrinsic 'quality', since these are critical judgements often made independently of personal satisfaction.

References   Barwise, P. and Ehrenberg, A. (1988) *Television and its Audience*. London: Sage.

Clausse, R. (1968) 'The mass public at grips with mass communication', *International Social Science Journal*, 20, **4**: 625–43.

Heeter, C. (1988) 'The choice process model', pp. 11–32 in Heeter C. and Greenberg B., *Cableviewing*. Hillsdale, NJ: Ablex.

Leggatt T. (1991) 'Identifying the undefinable', *Studies of Broadcasting*, **27**: 113–32.

Webster, J.G. and Wakshlag J.J. (1983) 'A theory of television program choice', *Communication Research*, 10, **4**: 430–46.

6 MEDIA ORGANIZATION, SELECTION AND PRODUCTION

6.1 THE MEDIA IN A FIELD OF SOCIAL FORCES

Research into media production has underlined the fact that most media organizations operate in an environment characterized by a high degree of public exposure and are subject to numerous, sometimes conflicting, demands from society, from their economic and commercial supports and partners and from their audience. Gerbner (1969) has portrayed mass communicators as operating under pressure from various external 'power roles', including clients (e.g. advertisers), competitors (other media), authorities (political and legal). We can add to these: investors; owners; other social institutions; the suppliers of content (news agencies, rights holders, etc., and advocates, pressure groups and public relations sources). Some of the authorities and influential social institutions have a dual power: they may have leverage in their own right and they may also be needed by the media as *sources* of news.

In addition, all media organizations are constrained by their actual or would-be audience. The degree of actual leverage and the balance of power varies from case to case, but the general situation of a media organization is one of continual potential conflict and pressure, often accentuated by the need to produce according to tight and inescapable deadlines. Figure 6.1.1 is intended to reflect these general conditions of media organizations, although it is drawn with news services (press or broadcasting) primarily in mind.

The figure illustrates the fact that a (news) media organization has to maintain relations with several sources of demand or constraint, especially: its audience; its owners; various social and political institutions (e.g., business firms, educational, health, political bodies); advertisers; potential suppliers of content (news and other agencies); regulatory agencies in the case of broadcasting. More 'distant' pressure may be exerted by financial institutions and society in general.

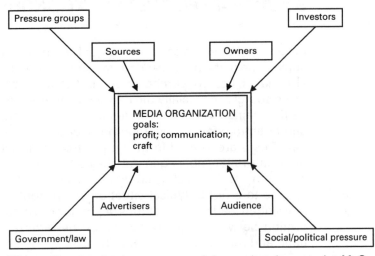

Fig. 6.1.1   The media organization: sources of demand and constraint McQuail 1987).

The relative significance of these relationships will vary according to the dominant goal of the media organization concerned. The main goals that have been identified are: making profits for owners or shareholders; some 'ideal purpose' (serving some cultural, social or political cause); maximizing and pleasing audiences; maximizing advertising revenue (Tunstall 1971). These goals often overlap, but rarely completely coincide. The fact that there are different external goals, also means that there will be different goals and work cultures within organizations, especially between those whose goals are: profit or management orientated, craft or technically orientated; or concerned primarily with communicative purposes (Engwall 1978).

References   Engwall, L. (1978) *Newspapers as Organizations.* Farnborough, Hants: Saxon House.

Gerbner, G. (1969) 'Institutional pressures on mass communicators' pp. 205–48 in Halmos, P. (ed.), *The Sociology of Mass Media Communicators. Sociological Review Monograph, 13.* University of Keele.

McQuail, D. (1987) *Mass Communication Theory,* 2nd edn. London: Sage.

Tunstall, J. (1971) *Journalists at Work.* London: Constable.

6.2 GIEBER AND JOHNSON'S MODEL OF SOURCE–REPORTER RELATIONSHIPS

Because of the typical news organization situation sketched above, one of the main issues in the study of media organizational conduct has concerned relations between media and their news sources, especially the degree of independence which can be maintained in the face of demands and pressures for access and attention, favourable treatment, or advertiser-friendly content. There are several forms and sources of potential pressure (McQuail 1992) and, in general, they add up to a threat to media autonomy and, possibly, credibility. The model described here applies to a not untypical situation where routine reporting of news often leads to, sometimes depends on, a measure of collaboration between regular sources or 'newsmakers' on the one hand and reporters on the other hand.

The authors of a study of reporter and source roles, Gieber and Johnson (1961), made use of some basic elements in the Westley and MacLean model (2.5) to illustrate some alternative possibilities in the relationship between reporters and sources, at least at the local community level.

The model can be presented in three parts, Figs 6.2.1, 6.2.2 and 6.2.3, each standing for one of the possibilities in the structure of the relationship. In each case, the symbol A is the source and corresponds to the A or 'advocate' in the model of Westley and MacLean, from which this model in part derives. The symbol C is the communicator role, in this case the reporter assigned to the 'City Hall beat'. The model derives from empirical research into the way the reporter covers news of local politics.

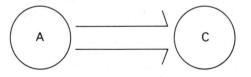

Fig. 6.2.1   Separate source-communicator roles (Gieber and Johnson 1961).

The relationship shown in Fig. 6.2.1 is described as follows by the authors: 'The communication acts of the two communicators, A and C, respectively, take place within frames of reference (the circles) separated by well differentiated bureaucratic functions, role assignments and perceptions, social distance, values, etc. The flow of information in channels (double line) tends to be formal.'

This model represents the classic case of a free press, in that there is assumed to be a complete independence between the social systems involved, the one 'making news', the other objectively reporting what happens. This case can apply in circumstances of distance and infrequency of contact between source and journalist.

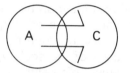

Fig. 6.2.2   Partially assimilated source and communicator roles (Gieber and Johnson 1961).

The relationship in Fig. 6.2.2 can be expressed as follows: The frames of reference of A and C overlap; the two communicators co-operate in achieving their communication roles and, in part, share the values underlying the communication roles and acts.

This version of the relationship is closer to what seems to happen in practice in such a relationship. The participants co-operate with each other and form a mutually agreed perception of their function. They have certain objectives in common, the one needing to get a particular story into a newspaper, the other needing to get news to satisfy an editor. The implication is that there will be some loss of independence by the C role, who should be acting as impartial agent of the public 'need to know'. Of the version as illustrated in Fig. 6.2.3 the authors say that 'The frame of reference for one communicator has been absorbed or otherwise taken over by the other; there is no distinction in role performance and values.' In principle, the model can accommodate a process of assimilation in either direction. It would be conceivable that a public official could supply information solely according to the demands and interests of the press. In reality, the pressure towards assimilation is nearly always in the other

Fig. 6.2.3   Assimilated source–communicator roles (after Gieber and Johnson 1961).

direction, since the supplier of information usually is in a stronger position in the relationship. The giving or withholding of news is a more effective sanction in day-to-day affairs than the longer-term sanction of inadequate or unfavourable publicity. The research example on which the model is based supports such an interpretation. Assimilation also occurs when the goals of the press are identified with the goals of the society, as in many socialist societies, or in circumstances of totalitarian or autocratic control.

Comment   The models should be taken as a whole as representing stages along a continuum of collaboration and assimilation which generally characterizes sources and news reporters. Apart from immediate work objectives of the reporter, the tendency to co-operate can be justified in terms of a general value of the 'good of the community' to which both source and local newspaper are likely to subscribe. Such a value penalizes conflict-orientated reporting or the retailing of 'negative' news about local officials and their activities. Hence collaboration does not derive from self-interest alone.

The model serves as a useful reminder that the 'gatekeeper' is part of a wider system of social relations and normative controls. It also captures the important fact that news does not simply flow into the impartial arms of the gatekeeper (as studies of telegraph editing seem to suggest). Rather, it is in some measure sought out and constructed in a bargaining relationship in which the work interests of participants, some of the goals of the original source and the assumed interests of the audience all play a part.

Several studies of news media have suggested that collaboration of the kind indicated does take place, although it normally falls short of full 'assimilation' (Sigal 1973; Chibnall 1975; Ericson *et al.* 1987; Murphy and Franklin, 1991). More often than not, it seems to result from of a combination of good public relations and information services on the source side, coupled with some laziness on the media side. The advantage for the media may also be a form of 'information subsidy'. It is a process which is more likely to occur at local and city level of media reporting (see Ericson *et al.* 1987; Fishman 1990) than at national level (Gans 1979). It is often a difficult matter to judge where cooperation shades into assimilation. In certain circumstances, authorities are in a very strong position to control access to scarce information with a high news value, and news media become assimilated, by necessity or choice, to official policy. This occurred, for instance in the cases of the Falklands and Gulf Wars.

References Chibnall, S. (1975) *Law and Order News*. London: Constable.
Ericson, R.V., Baranak, P.M. and Chan, J.B.L. (1987) *Vizualizing Deviance*. Toronto: University of Toronto Press.
Fishman, J. (1980) *Manufacturing the News*. Austin: University of Texas Press.
Gans, H.J. (1979) *Deciding What's News*. New York: Vintage Books.
Gieber, W. and Johnson, W. (1961) 'The City Hall beat: a study of reporter and source roles', *Journalism Quarterly*, **38**: 289–97.
McQuail, D. (1992) *Media Performance*. London: Sage.
Murphy, D. and Franklin, R. (1991) *What News? The Market, Politics and the Local Press*. London: Routledge.
Sigal, L.V. (1973) *Reporters and Officials*. Lexington, MA: D.C. Heath.

6.3 MEDIA GATEKEEPING

The concept of *gatekeeper* has been frequently used in studies of the mass communication process, especially, but not solely, with reference to any action within a media organization which involved choosing or rejecting some potential item for publication.

The concept originated in work carried out by Kurt Lewin (1947) dealing with decisions about household food purchases. He noted that information has always to flow along certain channels which contain 'gate areas', where decisions are made, either according to impartial rules or personally by a 'gatekeeper', as to whether information or goods will be allowed to enter in, or continue, in the channel. In a side reference, he invoked a comparison with the flow of news in mass communication. This idea was taken up and applied by White (1950) in a study of the telegraph wire editor of an American non-metropolitan paper, whose decision to discard many items was seen as the most significant gatekeeping activity. The model underlying this study can be expressed as in Fig. 6.3.1.

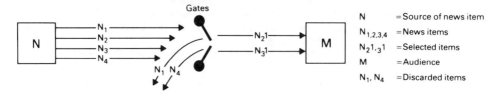

Fig. 6.3.1   White's simple gatekeeping model (based on White 1950).

This model has been extended and criticized in later work, although it has served as the basis for subsequent research into the process of selection from news agency copy. Chronologically, it was succeeded by the Westley and MacLean model (described above) which is also, amongst other things, a gatekeeper model and which tends to emphasize the system context in which gatekeeping takes place.

Comment   Apart from its obvious simplicity, there are a number of weaknesses in this original White model which have led to its modification or, for some purposes, replacement. Firstly, the model takes no account of organizational factors which constrain and direct the process and it lends itself to rather personalized interpretations of the activity being studied. Secondly, the model suggests there is only *one* main 'gate area'. Thirdly, the model implies a rather passive activity as far as the flow of news is concerned. There is an impression from the model, that there is a continuous and free flow of a wide range of news which has only to be tapped in ways which suit a particular newspaper. In spite of these criticisms, this conceptualization has been extremely influential in matters beyond the scope of the original research and White contributed a name to a whole school of research on communicators.

Gatekeepers in the media are not only selectors of news stories, but also cover a wider range of media occupational roles, for instance those of 'agent' for artists and writers, producer or promoter of cultural events, and book publishers (Hirsch 1977).

In a comprehensive overview of gatekeeping theory and research, Shoemaker (1991) has greatly extended the simple news gatekeeping shown above, to take account of the social system and the ideological and cultural context in which gatekeeping takes place. She also draws attention to the social and institutional factors at work (including sources, advertisers' markets, interest groups and government). In her account, gatekeeping often involves more than one communication organization (e.g., sources and news media as shown in 6.7 below) and multiple acts of gatekeeping take place within a media organization. These can be analysed at levels other than that of the individual – for instance as organizational routines. At each step in the process, selection tends to be heavily influenced by the anticipated selection criteria of the receiver. Some of these points are taken up in the models which follow and the reader can refer back to the Westley and MacLean model (2.5).

References   Hirsch, P.M. (1977) 'Occupational, organizational and institutional models in mass media research', pp. 13–42 in Hirsch, P.M., Miller, P.V. and Kline, F.G. (eds), *Strategies for Mass Communication Research*. Beverly Hills, CA: Sage.

Lewin, K. (1947) 'Channels of group life,' *Human Relations*, **1**: 143–53.
Shoemaker, P.J. (1991) *Gatekeeping*. Newbury Park, CA: Sage.
White, D.M. (1950) 'The "Gatekeepers": a case study in the selection of news'. *Journalism Quarterly*, **27**: 383–90.

6.4

McNELLY'S MODEL OF NEWS FLOW

An early point of criticism of the White model was that it showed only one gatekeeper rather than several, as one would normally expect to find in a complex news operation. McNelly's model (1959) is addressed to this particular problem, since it seeks to represent the various intermediary communicators standing between the event and the ultimate receiver (newspaper, reader, etc.).

The process which the model represents can be described in the following way, taking a hypothetical foreign news event. A

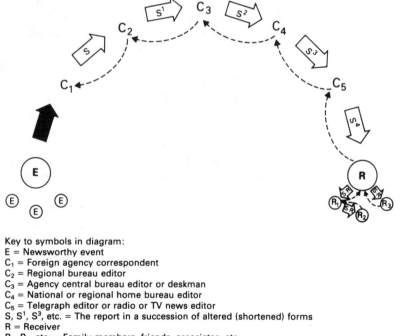

Key to symbols in diagram:
E = Newsworthy event
C_1 = Foreign agency correspondent
C_2 = Regional bureau editor
C_3 = Agency central bureau editor or deskman
C_4 = National or regional home bureau editor
C_5 = Telegraph editor or radio or TV news editor
S, S^1, S^3, etc. = The report in a succession of altered (shortened) forms
R = Receiver
R_1, R_2, etc. = Family members, friends, associates, etc.
$S - R$ = Story as modified by word of mouth transmission
Dotted line = feedback

Fig. 6.4.1 McNelly's model of intermediary communicators in news flow, showing news passing different 'gatekeepers' (McNelly 1959).

foreign news agency correspondent learns of a newsworthy event and writes a report which goes first to a regional bureau, from where it may be sent in shortened form to the agency central bureau. There, it may be combined with a related story from elsewhere and sent to a national or regional bureau of the country, where it may be again cut for transmission to the telegraph editor of a newspaper or radio/television station. Here it is further cut before it reaches the reader or listener. Further selection then occurs and the story may either be ignored or alternatively passed on by word of mouth to a succession of people. Throughout the process, various forms of feedback response occur which may guide further acts of transmission (see Fig. 6.4.1).

Comment   The important points emphasized by the model are:
1. the fact that the most important gatekeeping may well have been completed before the news reaches the telegraph editor of a newspaper, especially in the case of foreign news where global news decisions are made in the major bureaux of big telegraph services;
2. gatekeeping is much more than just selecting or rejecting, since the intermediaries often alter the form and substance of those stories that survive the journey;
3. gatekeeping does not end with the news medium, since the initial receiver often acts as gatekeeper for others;
4. feedback (broken lines in the diagram) is often infrequent and delayed.

The model is still in some respects incomplete in its own terms, since it could be extended at its initial stages. It tends to take 'newsworthiness' for granted and treats the agency correspondent as the primary source. There may well be two or three additional stages: there will be a witness to an event or one of the participants, thence often a local report, taken up by a stringer, and passed to the agency correspondent.

Reference   McNelly, J.T. (1959) 'Intermediary communicators in the international flow of news', *Journalism Quarterly*, **36**: 23–6.

6.5 BASS'S 'DOUBLE ACTION' MODEL OF INTERNAL NEWS FLOW

Bass (1969) in a revision of the gatekeeper theory suggests a simple but important elaboration of existing models. His main criticism of previous conceptualizations in both White and McNelly is that there is no differentiation between the roles of different 'gatekeepers' and no indication of what is the most significant point of selection. He argues that the most important gatekeeping activity occurs within the news organization and that the process should be divided into two stages, that of news *gathering* and news *processing*, as shown in Fig. 6.5.1.

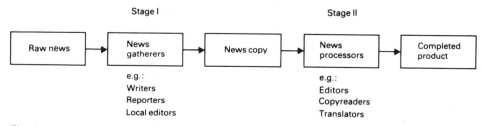

Fig. 6.5.1   News gathering and news processing are separate aspects of news production (Bass 1969).

The first step occurs when the news gatherers make 'raw news' – events, speeches and news conferences – into 'news copy' or news items. The second step occurs when the news processors modify and unify the items into the 'completed product' – a newspaper or a news broadcast – that is delivered to the public.

Comment   This model has been found useful in studies of journalistic activity (e.g. Tunstall 1971) and the two-fold division helps to separate those who are likely to be closest to sources and most orientated to them from those who are acting more literally in the gatekeeping sense by choosing, changing or excluding an incoming flow of content.

References Bass, A.Z. (1969) 'Refining the gatekeeper concept', *Journalism Quarterly*, **46**: 69–71.

Tunstall, J.T. (1971) *Journalists at Work*. London: Constable.

6.6   GALTUNG AND RUGE'S MODEL OF SELECTIVE GATEKEEPING

The model to be described here is not strictly an advance on, or development of, those gatekeeping models which have already been discussed. It rests on a relatively simple version of the flow of news and of gatekeeping as a process of successive selections according to a number of news values or criteria which affect the perception of news events.

For us, its main interest is that it develops in some detail one aspect of gatekeeping which is neglected or dealt with only in general terms by other models, namely the criteria which are applied in deciding whether to select or reject. If these criteria are completely subjective and vary from one gatekeeper to another, there is no point in considering them from the communication model perspective. However, there is reason to believe that the selection process is fairly systematic and in some degree predictable.

Galtung and Ruge approach the problem by naming and describing the main characteristics of an original news event which will influence its chances of being picked up initially and of passing the various gates, of the kind described in the McNelly model.

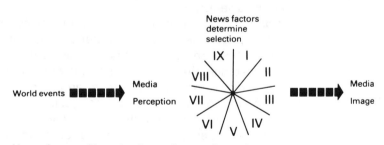

Fig. 6.6.1   News factors filter the flow of news (based on theory in Galtung and Ruge (1965)

The model in Fig. 6.6.1 represents the process by which world events are converted by media organizations into a 'media image' or picture of the world which is distributed to the audience. The application of the model to problems of explanation and prediction depends on a few basic hypotheses about the way in which these variables or 'news factors' alone or in combination affect selection and rejection.

The news factors are, briefly, as follows:

I.   *Timespan.* An event is more likely to be noticed if its occurrence fits the time schedule of the medium concerned. For instance, an event begun and completed in a few hours or less suits a daily newspaper or a news broadcast while a complex event taking several days to develop suits a weekly newspaper. Some events are too slow in developing, however important, to be really 'newsworthy' for the mass media.

II.   *Intensity or threshold value.* An event is more likely to be noticed if it is of great magnitude, or if its normal level of significance suddenly increases so as to attract particular notice. The latter applies where there is normally some surveillance by the media, e.g. of government or financial matters, or an ongoing conflict.

III. *Clarity/lack of ambiguity.* The less the meaning of an event is in doubt, the more likely it is to be suitable for news treatment.

IV.   *Cultural proximity or relevance.* The closer the event to the culture and interests of the intended audience, the more likely is selection.

V.   *Consonance.* An event which conforms to certain established expectations or preconceptions is more likely to be selected than one which does not conform to expectations. For instance, there are parts of the world where conflict is expected, some activities are inherently dangerous, others are associated with political change, etc.

VI.   *Unexpectedness.* Amongst events which are equally consonant in the sense of V, the more unusual and unpredictable the actual event, the more likely it is to be selected.

VII. *Continuity.* Once an event has been defined as newsworthy, there will be some momentum to the continued noticing of the event or related happenings.

VIII. *Composition.* News events are selected according to their place in a balanced whole (newspaper or newscast) and some events are consequently selected on grounds of contrast.

IX. *Sociocultural values* of the receiving society, or gatekeepers, will influence choice, over and above the news factors described.

There are three main hypotheses about the joint action of these news factors. Firstly, there is an *additivity* hypothesis which states that the more news factors are associated with a given event, the more likely it is to become 'news'. Secondly, there is a *complementarity* hypothesis which states that if an event is low on one factor it may compensate by being higher on some other factor. Thirdly, there is an *exclusion* hypothesis, according to which an event low on all factors will not become news.

The model is based on propositions from the psychology of individual perception. It is an important implication of the model and one reason for its influence, that the outcome of gatekeeping along these lines is to produce an ordered structure or image of the places, people and events in the news and, moreover, one which differs significantly and predictably from 'reality'. It is important to stress that the model only applies to foreign news, although a similar version of the theory could be developed for domestic news.

Comment   The approach described has been extremely influential in studies of news content and some confirmation is claimed on the basis of empirical testing (Galtung and Ruge 1965; Smith 1969; Sande 1971).

Rosengren (1974) mentions three main grounds of criticism. Firstly, it is too psychological, and depends too much on ideas about selective perception by individual gatekeepers. He recommends an alternative approach which takes more account of political and economic factors governing news reporting. In short, the set of news factors can be incomplete, without noting the particular circumstances of the political and economic relations between the countries concerned.

Secondly, Rosengren argues that the model is untestable and not open to falsification, because, taken together, the additivity and complementarity hypotheses can apply to all cases.

Thirdly, the model has not yet been adequately tested with an appropriate methodology. A satisfactory test would require reference to 'extra-media' data – evidence of other (e.g. political/economic) variables and also independent sources of knowledge about the 'reality' of events which were, or were not, covered. These criticisms leave open the possibility of an improvement in the explanatory power of the model by adding new variables and extending the methodology. A later application of the scheme to the analysis of news on Dutch television (Bergsma 1978) has cast some doubt on the general tenability of the complementarity hypothesis, but has shown the utility of the scheme in studying the operation of news values.

References   Bergsma, F. (1978) 'News values in foreign affairs on Dutch television', *Gazette*, **24**: 207–22.

Galtung, J. and **Ruge, M.H.** (1965) 'The structure of foreign news', *Journal of Peace Research*, **2**: 64–90.

Rosengren, K.E. (1974) 'International news: methods, data, theory', *Journal of Peace Research*, **11**: 145–56.

Sande, O. (1971) 'The perception of foreign news', *Journal of Peace Research*, **8**: 223–37.

Smith, R.F. (1969) 'On the structure of foreign news: a comparison of the *New York Times* and the Indian White Papers', *Journal of Peace Research*, **6**: 23–6.

6.7 SELECTION AND PRODUCTION SEQUENCE IN TWO DIFFERENT MEDIA

The models outlined above relate primarily to news media and news processing and focus on selected aspects of what occurs in or at the threshold of the news organization. In this section we look at a more complete model of a newspaper organization and its production process and also at a model which describes comparable features of the popular music industry.

6.7.1 Newsmaking

As part of their study of Canadian newspapers, Ericson *et al.* (1987), employed two main models, the first of which (Fig. 6.7.1) draws on elements in the Galtung and Ruge model just described. It shows how occurrences are transformed into the typical news 'event' content of a news medium by passing through a series of gates and filters, both on the side of the source and on the side of the medium. The model brings together several of the points already illustrated and it applies particularly to situations where there are established links between the institutions where 'news events' occur (e.g. legal or political bodies) and the news media.

The model portrays a two-stage process, involving source organizations and the news media. Within the source organization (for instance business firms, government departments, law-enforcement agencies), there is a pre-selection of events to present to the news media, filtered according to a set of news factors (some technical, others 'ideological') of the kind described by Galtung and Ruge (6.6). This process is carried out by specific 'source persons' who bring pressure on the media to pick up occurrences as potential news items. This is often part of a process of planned information, publicity and news management.

At the centre of the model, sources and reporters are shown to have a degree of shared interest in selecting and passing on certain 'source events' into the media production process (6.2. above). This takes place by way of one or other 'source medium' – the channel of communication from source organization to the media. Typical 'source media' are official reports, press releases,

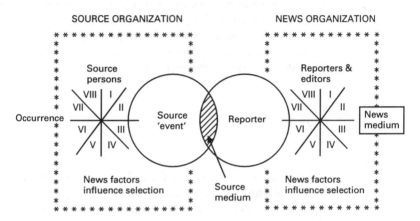

Fig. 6.7.1　　　Contexts of newsmaking (adapted from Ericson *et al.* 1987).

press conferences, telephone interviews, etc. However, news organizations will have different criteria of selection and different priorities from those of source organizations. Reporters and editors apply news factor criteria again before choosing what finally enters the medium in the form of news event accounts. This process within the media organization is similar to that represented by Bass's 'Double Action' model (6.5).

6.7.2　　　The news production process

A more complete model of the news production process and typical organizational chart is given in Fig. 6.7.2, enlarging what occurs within the right-hand side of Fig. 6.7.1.

The labels and arrows make the chart largely self-explanatory, but the following points should be noted.

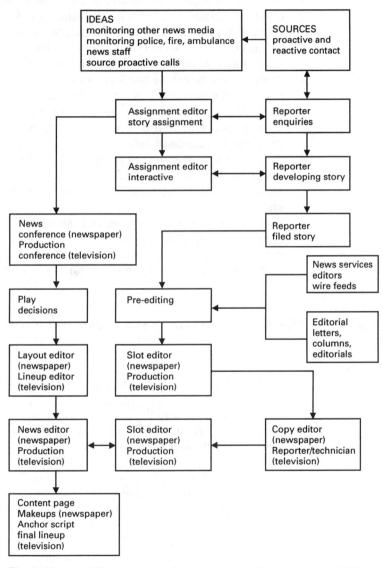

Fig. 6.7.2   The news production process (Ericson *et al.* 1987).

- Sources can be *proactive* (sought out by the media) or *reactive* (the case mainly described by Fig. 6.7.1).
- Ideas for content are actively canvassed and can cover diverse possibilities, although other media and regular sources figure prominently. Proactive ideas would involve initiative on the part of reporters or media and this has sometimes been described as 'enterprise reporting' (Sigal 1973).
- Assignment refers to the key act of allocating reporter resources to established or enterprise story possibilities.
- Conferences of editorial staff about news 'play', layout (newspaper) and lineup (television) play an important part in the daily sequence of selection.
- Some content is always readily available for use and within the control of the organization (news agency content, letters, editorials, syndicated columns, soft news, entertainments, etc.).
- In general, we see a continuous sequence from initiating content supply, through selection decisions and then to format, makeup, design and presentation decisions, where technical criteria are more important than editorial ones.

6.7.3 The decision chain in the music industry

An equivalent process in a different media industry is illustrated in Fig. 6.7.3.

The sequence through the many stages shown in the model is characterized by Ryan and Peterson in terms of a series of gates or filters at which decisions are made, often by different people with different skills. Their model is mainly intended to help understand the nature of those decisions. Link 1, between writer and publishing firm is mediated by agencies and many songs come from freelance writers already under contract. The supply is also strongly influenced by anticipated demand of the publishing firm. If a song is accepted, it is often rewritten and tried out before following link 2 to the recording stage. An important factor here is the choice of artist and songs are often changed again to suit the style or image of performance. Many songs do not proceed to the stage of release (3). After a release decision, decisions follow two lines simultaneously, one (4) concerning the form of marketing adopted, the other (5), manufacture and distribution.

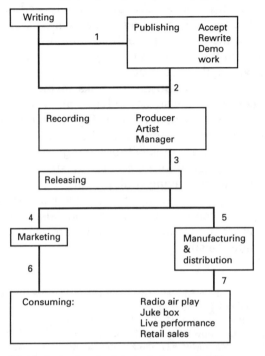

Fig. 6.7.3   Music industry decision chain model (Ryan and Peterson 1982).

What happens in both steps varies according to whether the publishing firm is a small independent or a large major. In the latter case, there will usually be an established route by way of the firms' own publicity and manufacturing divisions. In the case of an independent, both pathways are more problematic and variable. Finally, via links 6 and 7, there are paths to actual consumption. Notable here, in comparison with other media, is the variety of possible outlets and forms of consumption. The media product can be bought as a consumer item (disc, tape or video), listened to over the air or via a juke box, or experienced as a live concert.

The authors of the model, which they applied in a case study of country music, concluded that the factor most influential in guiding decisions and accounting for the consistency of decisions and connectedness of the chain is that of 'product image'. A musical product has to have a particular identity or image, which is attributed to the ultimate intended audience, but which, in any case, guides the selection and the reshaping of a particular song at each link in the organizational chain. Decision-makers aim to produce works 'that are much like the products that have most recently passed through all the links in the decision chain to become commercially successful' (p. 25).

This model is important not only for clarifying a very common media organizational tendency, but because such a loosely structured set of activities, often without a single organizational home, may become typical of other media industries. The 'phonogram' is characterized by having multiple forms of consumption, and this increasingly applies to other media. For instance, films are now not only seen in the cinema, but also bought over the counter as videos, rented out, shown on television and fed to cable or satellite subscribers.

References   Ericson, R.V., Baranak, P.M. and Chan, J.B.L. (1987) *Vizualizing Deviance*. Toronto: University of Toronto Press.

Ryan J. and Peterson R.A. (1982), 'The product image: the fate of creativity in country music songwriting', pp. 11–32 in Ettema J.S. and Whitney D.C. (eds), *Individuals in Mass Media Organizations*. Beverly Hills, CA: Sage Publications.

Sigal, L.V. (1973) *Reporters and Officials*. Lexington: D.C. Heath.

A great deal of communication that takes place every day falls under the label of planned communication; occasions when communication is consciously used to seek more or less specific objectives. Such communication may be planned to a greater or a lesser degree and may range from a purposive communication between two persons to a large-scale health campaign, involving several channels with many messages, aiming at millions of people. In this chapter we focus on three types of applied communication: media campaigns; public relations; and (social) marketing. In all three, mass communication usually plays an important part.

From our presentation of different models it may look as if campaigners and public relations practitioners work in very systematic and conscious ways. In everyday practice, however, communication is often based on vague and private theories and models, a mixture of personal experience, scientific or semi-scientific thinking and spur-of-the-moment reactions.

7.1   THE COMMUNICATION CAMPAIGN

Despite a great diversity of form, the communication campaign is often said to have the following characteristics:
- it has a collective, organized source;
- it is purposeful, guided by certain objectives, which may be very clearly specified;
- there may be multiple objectives within the same campaign, for instance of influencing attitudes, opinions or behaviour;
- it is to a large degree public in character, implying the use of mass media and accountability for aims, methods and effects;
- it usually involves more than one channel and more than one message, with mass communication supplemented by personal contact;
- it may be targeted to specific groups or to large publics, depending on the aims;
- a campaign is an institutionalized activity, which should be legitimate in the public eye, conform to established norms and not be too controversial.

Typical of campaigns in modern societies, leaving aside commercial advertising, have been those conducted by political parties and candidates for election, public health and safety campaigns, fund-raising activities for charities or disaster relief, etc.

Amongst several possible models for communication campaigns, we have chosen that of Nowak and Wärneryd (1985), which is a good example of the traditional type, starting as it does with the source's aim and ending with the effects achieved by the campaign. The model, graphically presented in Fig. 7.1.1 may be viewed as a description of the typical work process in campaigning. It also has a normative character in that it suggests how to work systematically in order to carry out an effective campaign.

An important idea underlying this model is that its elements are closely interrelated, such that a change in one element may cause change in others. This holds true especially when it comes to the intended effect (the aim) of the campaign. When the campaigner changes the aim, all or some of the other elements will be altered. Also, the better and more precisely the aim is stated, the fewer options the campaigner has in defining other elements. It is far from unusual for one to have to change the aim during the campaign, for example when certain channels or messages prove to be less effective than initially supposed. The elements pictured can be described as follows.

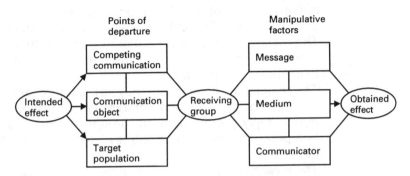

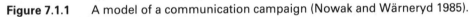

Figure 7.1.1   A model of a communication campaign (Nowak and Wärneryd 1985).

The intended effect: A major problem in many communication campaigns is that the goals (and related target groups) are not properly defined. The less good the goal definition, the smaller the chance to assess in the end whether the campaign has been successful or not. A common mistake in less sophisticated campaigns is vastly to overestimate the potential effects of a campaign.

Competing communication: It is important for the effectiveness of the campaign that it will not be disturbed by competing or even contradictory communication. The campaigner has to be aware of possible counter messages in order to address them properly.

The communication object: A campaign is usually centred around a theme or an object, such as a healthier life-style or drunken driving. Different objects require different modes of communication. On the other hand, the campaigner usually has several options when it comes to defining the object. For example, 'Aids' may be defined in a campaign as a disease of specific groups or one from which everyone is at risk. The emphasis might also be on its deadly character or on the potential for treatment.

The target population and the receiving group: The target population is here defined as all those whom the campaign is intended to affect. It is often, though not always, identical with with the intended receiving group. The sender may, for example, direct the message to a receiving group of 'opinion leaders' within the target population (3.2), with the intention of further dissemination amongst others. Target populations and receiving groups are sometimes classified according to ease or difficulty of reach. The most difficult groups in this respect are those who do not perceive the need for the message and are not normally exposed to communication channels.

The channel: As noted, there may be multiple channels for different types of message and different target groups. Mass media may initially put a theme on the agenda of discussion, while interpersonal communication may later be needed to influence behaviour.

The message: Typically, a central message can be shaped differently for different audiences. It may also change according to the stage of the campaign. For instance, an early stage may seek to develop awareness, while later stages seek to persuade or influence behaviour. A final phase may be designed to reassure those who have yielded to the campaign that they have acted wisely.

The communicator/sender: The communicator (spokesperson) can be chosen on several grounds: for instance as a trusted expert or because of potential attractiveness to the audience. Many campaigns use so-called pseudo-communicators, for example rock stars who are used to attack drug abuse because they are more likely to be listened to than the real source. As noted, legitimacy and credibility in the eyes of receivers are important source qualities in persuasion. The term 'sender' may be used to denote the person(s) or institution(s) that stand behind a message without being a spokesperson. The effectiveness of the whole campaign will benefit from the involvement of a legitimate and trustworthy sender.

Obtained effect: The effects of a campaign can be both intended and unintended, negative as well as positive. They can be cognitive (attention and knowledge gains), affective (relating to feelings, moods and attitudes) and conative (behaviour, activity and implementation). These different effects are often related to each other, although there is no fixed or unique sequence (see Section 7.3).

Reference   **Nowak, K.** and **Wärneryd, K.E.** (1985) *Kommunikation och åsiktförändring.* Stockholm: Prisma.

7.2 DIMENSIONS OF CAMPAIGN OBJECTIVES AND EFFECTS

Campaigns may vary widely in many respects and Rogers and Storey (1987) have summarized some important dimensions of difference, especially those that relate to objectives and effects, as shown in Fig. 7.2.1. The figure shows the intersection of three dimensions: one relating to the aims, another to the location of intended change (also indicating the level of analysis), a third to the balance between benefit for sender or receiver (locus of benefit). In effect, this leads to a three-fold typology of campaigns.

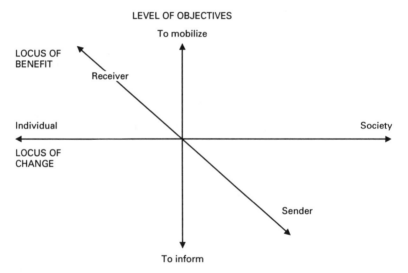

Figure 7.2.1   Dimensions of campaign objectives and effects (Rogers and Storey 1987).

Level of objectives: The different purposes of a campaign can often be ordered hierarchically or sequentially, for instance as follows: to gain attention; to influence attitudes; to affect behaviour in an intended way. Alternatively, they may be ordered in accordance with the stages of the innovation-diffusion process

(3.4): knowledge; persuasion; decision; confirmation. The idea behind such 'hierarchies of effects' (7.3) or similar sequences is that the fulfilment of an objective on one level usually requires that an effect on another, 'lower', level should have been reached. Rogers and Storey describe a pure *information campaign* as having an objective on a lower level than the *persuasion* campaign and yet lower than that of the *mobilization* campaign that has typically to build on prior changes (both of knowledge and attitude) in order to attain behavioural changes.

Locus of change: Usually communication campaign effects can be found on several levels: individual, group and societal, at the same time. It may be argued that changes sought on a societal level, such as lower national traffic accident rates, imply numerous individual changes in traffic behaviour. A campaigner may also try to bring about group changes in order to cause individuals to change, for instance in their food habits. The campaigner wanting, for example, to bring about a pervasive attitudinal change amongst the personnel of a large firm will have to decide whether to aim for individual or for group processes as the best means of influence.

Locus of benefit: Most campaigns are potentially beneficial to more than one of the parties involved (senders and receivers, a third party). The main purpose of a national health campaign, for example, is for the public to become more healthy and to live better. At the same time, the sender (the state) will benefit from lower costs for hospital care. A third party, employers, also stands to benefit from lower absenteeism at the workplace. Even a purely commercial campaign may be said to benefit the sender, who increases profits, and the customer, who may have been able to make a better-informed purchase. Nevertheless, there is often a basic difference between campaigns which primarily aim to benefit the initiator (as in advertising) and those which try to help the receiver (as with campaigns seeking to increase take-up of welfare benefits).

Reference   **Rogers, E.M.** and **Storey, J.D.** (1987) 'Communications campaigns', pp. 817–46 in Berger C.R. and Chaffee S.H. (eds), *Handbook of Communication Science.* Newbury Park, CA: Sage.

7.3   COMMUNICATION EFFECTS HIERARCHY

As noted above, communication campaigns can have different effects – especially on knowledge, attitudes or behaviour. Effects also occur in different degrees and sequences. Early studies of media effect (e.g. Hovland *et al.* 1949) concluded that planned communication first and foremost affects information, then attitudes and only later and in less degree, behaviour. However, it was noted that the relation between the three could change in the longer term. In an overview and comparison of effect theories, Ray (1973) concluded that there were three different basic models of effect hierarchy or sequence depending in the communication situation, as follows:

1. The learning hierarchy: cognitive, affective, behavioural.
2. The dissonance–attribution hierarchy: behavioural, affective, cognitive.
3. The low-involvement hierarchy: cognitive, behavioural, affective.

The learning hierarchy represents the classic case where subjects are exposed to a persuasive campaign in which there is a clear position presented or a clear choice between different alternatives. The audience is assumed to be motivated and interested and to proceed from learning about an idea or innovation, to developing favourable attitudes, to adaptation of behaviour. An earlier step was assumed to be a precondition for a subsequent one (hence the idea of a 'hierarchy' of effects). The case of innovation diffusion presented in 3.4 above fits this pattern.

The 'dissonance–attribution' hierarchy takes exactly the reverse sequence. Some new behaviour or experience (e.g., trying a new product or exposure to a powerful message stimulus) leads first to attitude change (an affective response), then to learning about the preference in order cognitively to support the behaviour (in line with balance and dissonance theory (2.4).

The 'low-involvement' hierarchy first developed by Krugman (1965) refers to a process in which the message offers little clear direction or chance of discrimination and the receivers are little interested or attentive. They pick up some information (e.g., about an available product), try it out (behaviour) and then adjust their attitude in line with the experience (again balance theory at work). According to Ray, it is typical of many television-viewing situations where attention is casual and effects may be subliminal. It is said to apply to television advertising, but it could have a wider application.

Chaffee and Roser (1986) have proposed a synthesis of the three models in a typical process of communication effect which is continuous and cumulative, and in which increasing involvement plays a key part, as shown in Fig. 7.3.1.

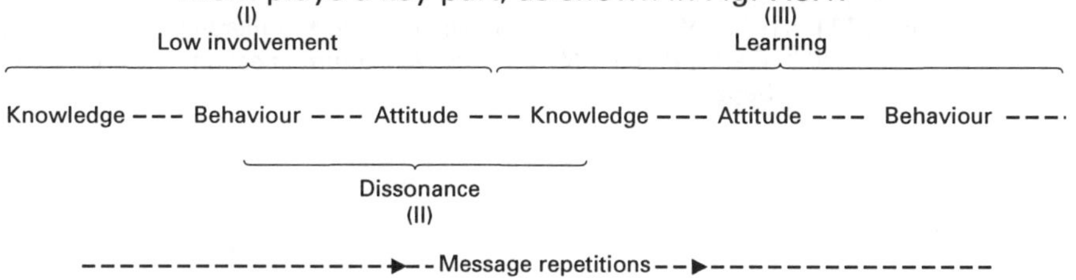

```
         (I)                                        (III)
   Low involvement                               Learning
 ┌──────────────────────┐           ┌────────────────────────────────┐

Knowledge --- Behaviour --- Attitude --- Knowledge --- Attitude --- Behaviour ---·

          └────────────────────┘
                Dissonance
                   (II)

        --------------->-- Message repetitions --►---------------
```

Fig. 7.3.1   Integrated model of effect hierarchies (Chaffee and Roser 1986).

Briefly put, they suggest that the earliest stage in a communication effect process (for instance in the case of a health campaign) follows the 'low-involvement model', as indicated. The receiver has little information and interest. However, a small amount of information is acquired leading to some behaviour change (e.g., trying a health practice), leading to more involvement. Values and behaviours in their turn become established and the person's method of responding to new information becomes more rational. The 'dissonance model' takes over, with more search for information, until the stage of 'learning model' is reached and receiver behaviour eventually becomes a reasoned response to what is known and felt, rather than an unthinking response. According to the authors, as a person follows the sequence shown in Figure 7.3.1 under the influence of message repetition, both knowledge and attitude change qualitatively, so that shallow and easily forgotten information develops into a reasoned set of ideas. These will be stable, consistent and good predictors of future behaviour. Key factors in the process will be continued exposure to information and increasing involvement. Without these, the process is likely to stop or not develop fully.

Chaffee and Roser tested the theory in relation to a health campaign and concluded that, in general, involvement is a condition for consistency between knowledge, attitudes and behaviour.

References   Chaffee, S. and Roser, C. (1986) 'Involvement and the consistency of knowledge, attitudes and behaviour', *Communication Research*, **3**: 373–99.

Hovland, C.I., Lumsdaine, A.A. and Sheffield, F.D. (1949) *Experiments on Mass Communication*. New York: John Wiley.

Krugman, H.E. (1965) 'The impact of television advertising', *Public Opinion Quarterly*, **29**: 349–56.

Ray, M.L. (1973) 'Marketing communication and the hierarchy of effects', pp. 147–76 in Clarke, P. (ed.), *New Models for Communication Research*. Beverly Hills, CA: Sage.

7.4   FOUR MODELS OF PUBLIC RELATIONS

Public relations is a growing field for applied communication in most countries. Of the several definitions of public relations, one of the simplest is that offered by Grunig and Hunt (1984, p. 8): 'Public relations . . . is the management of communication between an organization and its publics.'

An organization may be a large corporation, a labour union or a major sports club. In modern public relations theory, the groups, institutions, etc., with which the organization communicates are called publics. These publics may be found within as well as outside the organization – for instance the employees as well as the clients of a business firm. Communication in public relations can be of many kinds. For some practitioners, goals are mainly to be reached through one-way processes, for some by two-way (interactive) ones. Most frequently, mixed strategies are chosen, depending on the situation at hand.

Grunig and Hunt (1984) maintain that it is possible to describe the historical development of PR strategies through four basic models. Although their description depicts the case of the United States, the four models can be found in all countries where public relations have developed. That the practitioners have been working according to certain *models* does not necessarily mean that they have been conscious of the theoretical base or of the principal differences between using one model or another.

The first to appear in American PR history is the *agent–publicity* model, in which propaganda is the main purpose of communication. It appeared in the latter part of nineteenth century. A newspaper claiming to its readership and advertisers to be the most popular or the 'best' may serve as an example. At the beginning of this century, the *public information* model appeared, with its main focus on the dissemination of information, for example, through company newsletters with the aim of reporting to employees in a more or less neutral way, on what is happening in the corporation. The ultimate aim would be to improve the reputation of the company with its staff.

In the 1920s, the *two-way asymmetric* PR model began to be

used; its aim was persuasion, often based on communication principles developed in communication science. An example of this could be a political party that effectively secures the placing of positive news stories in the press. This is a way of managing response from the society and from the intended public of potential voters. The self-interested organization maintains firm control.

Much later, in the 1960s, the *two-way symmetric* model came into use, stressing mutual understanding as a goal and involving genuine efforts to exchange views and information with the relevant public. This strategy may, for example, be used by a local school that keeps up a dialogue with different groups in the community such as parents and political groups, who may or may not support the school.

These different models are represented graphically in Figs. 7.4.1 to 7.4.4. The agent–publicity model shown in Fig. 7.4.1 is an extreme example of a one-way process, in which truth is not essential and the communication content is intended to persuade simply by its prominence, or repetition or wide appeal. The initiative is always strongly in the hands of the source/sender. The means are usually straightforward advertising or various other forms of promotional activity.

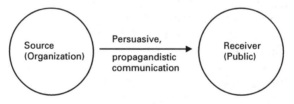

Fig. 7.4.1   The agent/publicity model (Grunig and Hunt 1984).

The public information model, as shown in Fig. 7.4.2, is built on the assumption that an organization should communicate truthful information to its public(s) in a one-way process, but not necessarily with persuasive intent. Large organizations usually develop their own information offices and maintain relations with mass media for these purposes.

The two-way asymmetric model (Fig. 7.4.3) describes a process where the sender/source intends to persuade its public, but since the source needs information about the communication needs of its publics in order to communicate more efficiently,

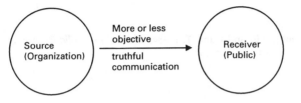

Fig. 7.4.2   The public information model.

feedback and 'feedforward' become essential. 'Feedforward' refers to the information a sender has about the audience before communicating. In terms of power and initative-taking, the source can be said to dominate the relationship.

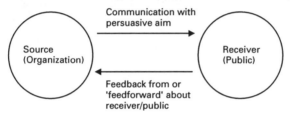

Fig. 7.4.3   The two-way asymmetric model

The two-way symmetric model (Fig. 7.4.4) depicts a communication relationship where the sender/source and the public(s) share initiative and power more equally. This PR model may be

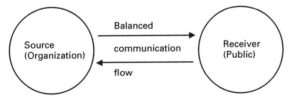

Fig. 7.4.4   The two-way symmetric model.

especially relevant when the aim is to solve problems and to avoid conflicts and where a lasting communication relationship is one of the requirements, rather than an *ad hoc* campaign.

As noted at the outset, few organizations stick to just one of these models in their public relations, but use different models for different purposes, in different situations.

Reference   **Grunig, J.E.** and **Hunt, T.** (1984) *Managing Public Relations.* New York: Holt, Rinehart and Winston.

7.5

MARKETING COMMUNICATION

In many processes of influence, the use of mass communication to inform or persuade a general public is usually only one element in a broader process. This applies to campaigns for health and safety, law enforcement, politics and commercial promotion. In many such cases, advertising is one important element, but successful campaigning requires other stages to be followed. Although the 'end consumers' play the most decisive role, the process of 'selling' products, ideas or candidates depends on a number of intermediaries and 'gatekeepers' (6.3). The gatekeepers may be housewives, buyers in organizations, retailers, opinion leaders, etc. Marketing refers to a set of promotional activities which involves communication to these intermediary decision makers as well as to potential direct consumers. Some marketing activities are not strictly communicative, but involve attention to what has been referred to as the Four P's (McCarthy 1975). These are: Product; Price; Place; Promotion; to which has been added a fifth, namely, Positioning.

These concepts are not only applicable to commercial marketing. There is a growing interest in using marketing concepts and thinking in non-commercial settings (Solomon 1989). Such so-called 'social marketing' has been defined as 'the design, implementation and control of programs seeking to increase the acceptability of a social idea, cause, or practice in a target group' (Kotler and Armstrong 1989). Social marketing models have been widely used, for instance, in health campaigns throughout the world or for raising money for good causes.

The five elements in marketing strategies can be described as follows.

The product may be differentiated and shaped in order to fit a specific market. The marketing communicator often puts much effort into defining the product in the way that will interest the potential buyer. A car may be presented in one market as a safe car, in another as fast and exciting. The appeal of a political candidate is also manipulated, where possible, according to the likely appeal to different segments of the electorate. The differentiation of product 'image' may be managed by the choice of different media channels.

The price. Marketers know that there are several ways of defining the price of a product. In addition to price in money terms, there can be social and psychological costs and benefits. A low-price product may entail a 'social' price, e.g., because of the stigma of cheapness. Health or safety practices may also carry social costs (e.g., reporting diseases) which have to be dealt with in campaigns. Giving to charities costs money but compensations can be pointed to by fund-raising campaigners.

Place refers to the type of channel through which the product or service is made available to the target group. Marketing communication will aim to make this channel as visible and known as possible. It may be important to choose a place of delivery which is suitable for the given product. A medicine, for instance, may be taken more seriously if it is made available through officially approved pharmacies. Charitable campaigns like to enlist trusted institutions such as banks as agents for collecting donations.

Promotion refers to the various communication activities such as advertising campaigns designed to increase awareness, knowledge and motivation to buy the product or service. According to Solomon (1989, p. 93), to promote means 'actively reaching out to the right people with the right message at the right time to obtain the right effects'. It is important to note that advertising, which is what the 'end consumer' may see as the most important part of promotion, often constitutes only a very small part of the whole range of activities aimed at getting the product or service accepted.

Positioning refers to the relationship between elements in the marketing field. Brand names or particular products are often positioned relative to competitors, e.g. as 'luxurious' or 'economical'. In social marketing, campaigners have to be aware of alternative efforts towards similar ends or potentially competing appeals. In democratic political *campaigning*, an element of positioning is central to the whole process.

Additional elements of the marketing process are those of *exchange* and *competition*. The first refers to the fact that any promotional effort should aim to meet needs and wants and respond to feedback from would-be consumers. Competition refers to the fact that most services and products are presented in a competitive environment and have to be differentiated and positioned in the most favourable ways possible. These two elements underline the need for information about the market and about potential competitors.

In Fig. 7.5.1 marketing strategy is presented, in the light of these comments, as a series of key moments at which decisions are taken by certain actors. The *source* of the marketing effort is an organization which may be assisted by an advertising agency, and which has to take decisions in the following sequence:

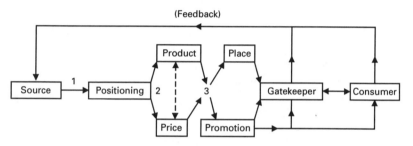

Fig. 7.5.1   Marketing strategy decision sequence and feedback.

1. Where to *position* itself or the product, service, candidate or appeal.
2. How to package, design, define and *price* the *product*.
3. How to *promote* the product and arrange distribution channels (*place*) in order best to reach and persuade gatekeepers and consumers.

The *gatekeepers* in the model can be of different kinds: buyers; retailers; social influentials; health professionals; household budget controllers, etc.

The *consumers* may often be reached by the promotion directly and may often act without gatekeepers as intermediaries. For the marketer it is of great importance to receive informational feedback from gatekeepers and consumers. This comes mainly in the form of sales figures (or the equivalent evidence – voting, service take-up) or market research.

References   **Kotler, P.** and **Armstrong, G.** (1989) *Principles of Marketing*. 4th edn. London: Prentice Hall International.

McCarthy, E.J. (1975) *Basic Marketing: a Managerial Approach*. Homewood: Irvin.

Solomon, D.S. (1989) 'A social marketing perspective on communication campaigns' in Rice, R.E. and Atkin, C. (eds), *Public Communications Campaigns*, 2nd edn. Newbury Park, CA: Sage.

8 NEW MEDIA AND THE INFORMATION SOCIETY

8.1 THE INFORMATION SOCIETY: PROMISE AND PROBLEMS

The concept 'information society' seems to have originated in Japan (Ito 1981), although it is a logical extension of earlier ideas about the rise of a 'post-industrial' society (Bell 1973) – one in which manufacturing gives way to service industry as the basis of the economy. Melody (1990, p. 26) defines an information society as one that has 'become dependent upon complex electronic information and communication networks and which allocates a major portion of resources to information and communication activities'.

Mass communication is only one element in the economy of information societies, but an important one, especially because of the accompanying production of electronic hardware and because of the increasing social and political significance of mass media. The development of new technologies of distribution (cable, satellite, etc.) and of interactive media such as videotex has led to a 'convergence' of modes and channels of communication (Pool 1983) which increasingly blurs the difference between public and private communication.

So far only a small number of the most developed countries can be said to have entered an 'information age' and the implications of the latent 'communications revolution' are still unclear. Commentators have, however, pointed to several potentially problematic consequences and to other effects which can be beneficial. It is far from clear that an information society will be a more informed society, or that people can cope with the vast amount of new information which is now produced and distributed (the so-called 'information overload'). On the positive side, for example, two-way interactive communication can replace the one-way flow characteristic of the mass media age. A consequence with mixed benefits and costs is the increased internationalization of communication made possible by the new technologies and new media industries (Ferguson 1992). Some predict a shared global community, others a more homogenized world, controlled by a few powerful centres and cultures (or corporations) (see also 4.6). A similar ambivalence attaches to the claim that new communication technology can overcome the old barriers of time and place. These are some of the issues which the models described in this and the following chapter aim to deal with.

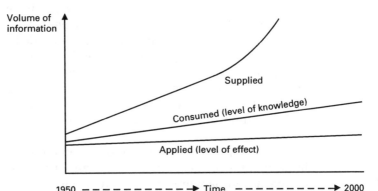

Fig. 8.1.1   Information flow and take-up (van Cuilenburg 1987).

The information and media 'abundance' which is one result of the communications revolution has been mainly caused by an enormous and very rapid increase in productivity as a result of miniaturization and computerization. The unit *cost* of production and transmission of information has fallen, leading to an exponential growth of supply of certain media and types of communication, especially in telecommunications and broadcasting. Print and mail media have become relatively more expensive, although supply has also grown along with economic activity (Ito, 1981). The capacity to produce information has far outstripped the human capacity to receive and process information. This has led to oversupply and sometimes to 'overload' and to organizational and personal inefficiency. This situation is captured in the graph (Fig. 8.1.1) showing the relation between information production, consumption and application or effect.

This figure shows three essential trends of the information society:

- Increased *supply* of information. Various estimates from different countries (see Pool *et al.* 1984) indicate that supply is growing at a steady annual rate of 8–10 per cent. More and more organizations and individuals are able to send information over considerable distances at lower cost.

- Information *consumption* is growing, but much more slowly, as measured by the amount of information received or attended to. In effect this means that demand for information lags behind supply, for a mixture of reasons, including limited processing capacity and resources.

- Information *application or effect* seems to be more or less constant, although it is much more difficult to measure. There are limits to the utility of additional information and oversupply is itself a cause of waste and confusion.

The situation is characterized by an unsustainable imbalance between supply and demand. Van Cuilenburg has compared the undirected flow of information to the situation of the 'blind round' in artillery which goes astray and often does not explode. From the point of view of the receiver or user of information, 'overload' refers to increased difficulty in finding useful or suitable information amongst a large supply, confusion and inconsistency, increased difficulty and cost in processing and storing information. The law of diminishing returns applies strongly to the information case. The gap between information supply and demand also accounts for the fact that the information society is not the same thing as a more informed society. The necessary conditions for the latter would include the better development of motivation and human communication potential.

The situation of high information supply can also be seen in a positive light. There is more choice, at lower cost, for information consumers and more possibilities for access to communication channels. The growing excess of supply over demand does not have to be harmful and may gradually be corrected by (for instance) a relatively more interactive and point-to-point communication flow (necessarily more balanced) and by improvements in information management (storage, replacement, access) (see the next section).

References   Bell, D. (1973) *The Coming of Post-Industrial Society*. New York: Basic Books.

van Cuilenburg, J.J. (1987) 'The information society: some trends and implications', *European Journal of Communication*, 2, **1**: 105–21.

Ferguson, M. (1992) 'The mythology about globalization', *European Journal of Communication*, 7, **1**: 69–94.

Ito, Y. (1981) 'The "Johoka Sakai" approach to the study of communication in Japan', in Wilhoit, G.C and de Bock, H. (eds), *Mass Communication Review Yearbook 2*. Beverly Hills, CA: Sage.

Melody, W. (1990) 'Communication policy in the global information economy', pp. 16–39 in Ferguson, M., (ed.), *Public Communication: the New Imperatives*. London: Sage.

Pool, I. de sola (1983) *Technologies of Freedom*. Harvard, MA: Belknap Press.

Pool, I. de sola, Inose, H., Takasaki, N. and Hunwitz, R. (1984) *Communication Flows: a Census in the US and Japan*. Amsterdam: North Holland

8.2 CHANGING BALANCE OF INFORMATION TRAFFIC

The new electronic media (sometimes called 'telematic' media because they combine telecommunications and informatics) have been defined as 'a set of services . . . which can be provided to the users by the telecommunications net and which allow public and private information and data to be sent and received' (Mazzoleni 1986, p. 100). The archetypal new telematic medium has the general name 'videotex' and involves a service, delivered by the telephone network, which enables individuals to consult and interact at will with data banks as well as with all other individuals connected to the net. The most essential capacity is that of *interaction* (Rogers 1986). There are more 'passive' forms of telematic media, such as teletext, which provide a large amount of broadcast (or cabled) information, from which a user can select according to wish or need. The number of electronic consultative media forms is increasing as are the possibilities for interpersonal interaction (electronic mail, telefax, teleconferencing, mobile phones, etc.). In principle, the changes promote a shift from mass media to small-scale media and of control from sender to receiver.

A useful way of considering the implications of these changes is to think in terms of alternative types of *information traffic* and the balance between them. Two Dutch telecommunication experts, J.L. Bordewijk and B. van Kaam (1982, 1986) have developed a model which helps to make clear and to investigate the changes under way. They describe four basic communication patterns and show how they are related to each other.

1. The allocution pattern (Fig. 8.2.1)

In this case, information is distributed from a centre simultaneously to many peripheral receivers. This pattern applies to several cases, ranging from a lecture, church service or concert (where listeners or spectators are physically present in an auditorium) to the situation of broadcasting, where radio or TV messages are received by large numbers of scattered individuals at the same moment. Allocution (a word derived from the Latin for the address by a Roman general to assembled troops) is typically *one-way* communication to many, with relatively little personal 'feedback' opportunity (especially in the mass media situation). Another characteristic is that time and place of communication are determined by the sender or at the 'centre'.

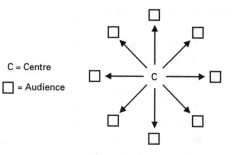

C = Centre

☐ = Audience

Fig. 8.2.1   Allocution.

2. The conversation pattern (Fig. 8.2.2)

Here, individuals (in a potential communication network) interact directly with each other, bypassing a centre or intermediary and choosing their own partners as well as the time, place and topic of

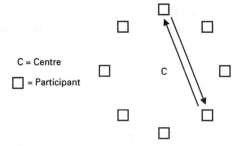

C = Centre

☐ = Participant

Fig. 8.2.2   The conversation pattern.

communication. This pattern also applies in a wide range of situations, from that of an exchange of personal letters to use of electronic mail. The electronically mediated conversation does, however, often imply a 'centre' or intermediary (such as the telephone exchange), even if this plays no active or initiatory role in the communication event.

Characteristic of the conversational pattern is the fact that parties are equal in the exchange. In principle, more than two can take part (e.g. a small meeting or telephone conference). However, at some point, increased scale of participation leads to a merger with the allocutive situation.

3. Consultation (Fig. 8.2.3)

This pattern also refers to a range of different communication situations in which an individual (at the periphery) looks for information at a central store of information – data bank, library, reference work, computer disc, etc. As noted, the possibilities are increasing. In principle, the pattern can also apply to the use of a newspaper (otherwise considered as an allocutive mass medium), since the time and place of consultation and also the topic are determined by the receiver at the periphery and not by the centre. In Fig. 8.2.3, the dotted line indicates the 'request' for information and the solid line the flow in response.

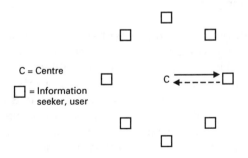

Fig. 8.2.3 The consultation pattern.

4. Registration (Fig. 8.2.4)

This pattern of information traffic is, in effect, the consultation pattern in reverse in that a centre 'requests' and receives information from a participant at the periphery. This applies wherever central records are kept of individuals in a system and to all systems of surveillance. It relates, for instance, to the automatic recording at a central exchange of telephone calls, to electronic alarm systems, to automatic registration of television set usage in 'people-meter' audience research, or for purposes of charging consumers. The accumulation of information at a centre often takes place without reference to, or knowledge of, the individual. While the pattern is not historically new, the possibilities for registration have increased enormously because of computerization and extended telecommunication connections. Typically, in this pattern, the centre has more control than the individual at the periphery to determine the content and occurrence of communication traffic.

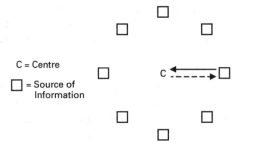

C = Centre

☐ = Source of Information

Fig. 8.2.4   The registration pattern.

These four patterns complement and border upon (or overlap with) each other. The authors of the model have shown how they can be related in terms of two main variables: of *Central versus Individual control* of information; and of *Central versus Individual control* of time and choice of subject (see Fig. 8.2.5).

The allocution pattern stands for typical 'old media' of communication – especially broadcasting, where a limited supply of content was made available to a mass audience. The consultation pattern has been able to grow, not only because of new telematic media, but because of the diffusion of video and sound-recording equipment and the sheer increase in the number of channels as a result of cable and satellite. The new media have also differentially increased the potential for 'conversational' or interactive communication between widely separated individuals. As noted, 'registration' becomes both more practicable and more likely to occur, although it is not a substitute for other types of communication traffic.

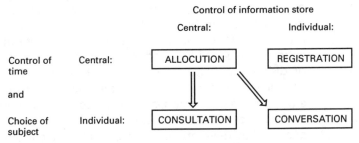

Fig. 8.2.5   A typology of information traffic (Bordewijk and van Kaam 1982, 1986).

The arrows in Fig. 8.2.5 reflect the redistribution of information traffic from allocutory to conversational and consultative patterns. In general, this implies a broad shift of balance of communicative power from sender to receiver, although this may be counterbalanced by the growth of registration. Allocutory patterns have not necessarily diminished in volume, but they have taken new forms, with more small-scale provision for segmented audiences based on interest or information need (narrowcasting). Finally, we can conclude from Fig. 8.2.5 that patterns of information flow are not so sharply differentiated as it might appear, but are subject to overlap and convergence, for technological as well as social reasons. The same technology (e.g. the telecommunications infrastructure) can provide a household with facilities for each of the four patterns described.

References   Bordewijk, J.L. and **van Kaam, B.** (1982) *Allocutie*. Baarn: Bosch and Kenning.

Bordewijk, J.L. and **van Kaam, B.** (1986) 'Towards a classification of new tele-information services', *Intermedia*, 14,1: 16–21.

Mazzoleni, G. (1986) 'Mass telematics: facts and fiction', pp. 100–14 in McQuail, D., and Siune, K. (eds) *New Media Politics*. London: Sage.

Rogers, E.M. (1986) *Communication Technology: The New Media in Society*. New York: Free Press.

8.3 CONVERGENCE OF COMMUNICATION MODES AND MODELS OF MEDIA REGULATION

Most public communication systems are regulated for reasons of the 'public interest' in order to meet some greater or longer-term objective of society, to ensure efficiency, quality and universality of service or protection of the consumer under conditions of monopoly. Three main models of regulation of public communication have been identified, each based on different technologies of distribution and/or reception. These are: the print model; broadcasting (public over-air transmission) of radio and television; and the common carrier model (for telecommunications and mail services). The main features are described below. It seems that developments of electronic technology (a convergence of modes of distribution in particular) are leading to a breakdown of the traditional barriers between the main types of media, thus making obsolete or inconsistent the distinctions between the established regulatory models (Pool 1983). The four types of information traffic just described (Section 8.2) can be used to compare the models and to analyse the changes under way. The print model is closest to the consultation pattern, the broadcasting model to allocution, the common carrier model to both conversation and registration.

Broadcast model. Reasons of scarcity and efficiency initially led to monopoly conditions and close control. Content has also been regulated for reasons of public interest (equity of access and control of effects). Reception is open to all, fulfilling a principle of universality of service.

Print media model. Typically, there is no, or only minimal control of technology, content or of the market which governs product supply and demand in respect of information. The essence of the model is maximum freedom. While 'sender access', as shown, is open to all in principle, in practice there are often high economic barriers to entry as print publishers.

Common carrier model. Infrastructure is closely controlled because telephone cable networks are usually natural monopolies, in which the consumer benefits from there being a single (local) supplier. However, content is not regulated, for reasons of

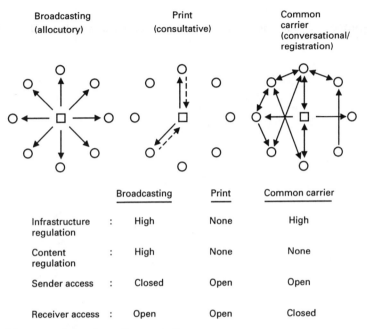

		Broadcasting	Print	Common carrier
Infrastructure regulation	:	High	None	High
Content regulation	:	High	None	None
Sender access	:	Closed	Open	Open
Receiver access	:	Open	Open	Closed

Fig. 8.3.1   Three models of media regulation.

individual privacy, since most traffic is 'point to point' between private individuals and organizations (e.g., conversations and data transmissions). Access as sender is universally and equally open, but for reasons of message privacy, reception is restricted to those addressed.

These regulatory models have co-existed for more than 50 years but are looking increasingly inconsistent and obsolete, for the reasons given. Most vulnerable to change and challenge is the broadcast model, since the grounds for monopoly regulation (especially channel scarcity) have largely disappeared and the legitimacy and necessity of control of content and access have been strongly challenged. In addition, many former broadcast services can now be distributed by telecommunications media, which have no comparable controls on content. Some reasons for regulation remain, however, on grounds of wider social purpose and consumer protection (in general, the public interest).

Reference   Pool, I. de sola (1983) *Technologies of Freedom.* Harvard, MA: Belknap Press.

8.4 COMMUNICATION POLICY AND SOCIAL PROBLEMS: CROSS-SYSTEM DIFFERENCES

The rise of communication to greater significance in modern societies has made it a more salient object of policy. The information society has been characterized as giving rise to a range of relatively novel social problems. These include the following:
- the invasion of (and need to protect) privacy;
- the misuse of information;
- maintaining social control;
- informational inequality;
- information monopoly;
- pornography;
- information overload.

However, the recognition and actual definition of these as problems varies according to political and economic circumstances and types of social system. Salvaggio (1985) proposes a four-fold distinction between types of society as follows: competitive (free market); public utility (mixed, or social-market economies as in West Europe); communist (as in the former USSR and still in China); Third World (most developing countries). His main point is that basically the same set of factors determines the relation between communication technology and social problems, but in different combinations and with varying priority. Two factors are especially important in all societies: one a *constant* factor of ideology (although *actual* reigning ideologies vary and change); the other a variable factor (X), which is different in each type of society. The resulting model is shown in Fig. 8.4.1.

The model identifies which variable is most likely to correspond to X in each of the four types of society, as follows: economic forces in free-market based systems; a policy body (such as a PTT or Ministry) under the public utility model; a political party in communist systems; and in the case of Third-World countries, external forces, meaning in practice that problems are outside national control. The model is a reminder of the variable and relative nature of the problems of an information society. Their nature, degree and recognition varies and so does the possibility for finding solutions.

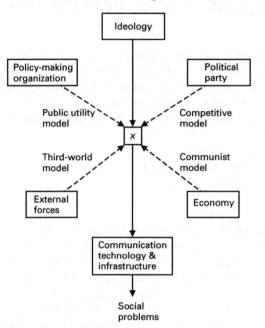

Fig. 8.4.1   Comparative system communication policy model (adapted from Salvaggio 1985).

Reference   **Salvaggio, J.L.** (1985) 'Information technology and social problems', pp. 428–54 in Ruben, B.D., (ed.), *Information and Behavior*, vol. 1. Rutgers, NJ: Transaction Books.

9 INTERNATIONAL COMMUNICATION

9.1 INTRODUCTION

The growing informatization of society has been accompanied by an extending and increasing international flow of communication and by greater cross-cultural influences. Technologies of electronic communication may have contributed most to the internationalizing process, but they have been abetted by several other trends: the extension of multinational business empires; attempts by competing power blocs to spread their power and influence; the rise of an international 'media culture' in which certain formats, languages and types of story have come to find wide acceptance in many different societies. The internationalization of communication is a symptom, reflection and also an instrument of the dissemination of a particular type of 'modern' culture and way of life.

Internationalization has been both celebrated and problematized. In more optimistic days, immediately after the Second World War, international communication was viewed as a means toward achieving greater international understanding and as an instrument of modernization and nation-building. It could supposedly transmit the culture of material progress and individualist democracy to traditional societies (Lerner 1958). Optimism was gradually replaced by a perception that international communication lent itself more to neo-colonialism than to growth and liberation. The perceived effects of the international flow of communication included diminished sovereignty and autonomy in cultural matters and increased economic and political dependency. The central fact had to be recognized that 'free' international communication in the modern world was bound to be unequal and one-directional, from rich to poor and from north to south. The poorer, less, developed countries are impelled to import the technology, structures, professional practices from the developed world (Boyd-Barrett 1977). Along with this came culturally alien world views and negative self-perceptions. The term 'cultural imperialism' (see Tomlinson 1991) was often heard to sum up the aim or tendency of internationalization. More recently, there has been concern within the 'First World' about increased cultural homogeneity and loss of national and regional identities as a result of accelerating technological and commercial developments in communication. The models which are described in this chapter tend to reflect the more pessimistic views mentioned although they also lend themselves to the empirical study of what is going on, which may not all be bad.

References   Boyd-Barrett, O. (1977) 'Media imperialism' in Curran J. *et al.*, (eds), *Mass Communication and Society*. London: Edward Arnold.
Lerner, D. (1958) *The Passing of Traditional Society*. New York: Free Press.
Tomlinson, J. (1991) *Cultural Imperialism*. London: Pinter.

9.2   INTERNATIONAL FLOW OF INFORMATION

Mowlana (1985) made a general analysis of all forms of international communication (of which mass communication may only be a minor element) and drew a model in which two dimensions are shown to be determinant for the issues introduced above. These are the technology axis (hardware versus software) and the communication axis (production versus distribution). The main features of the model appear in Fig 9.2.1.

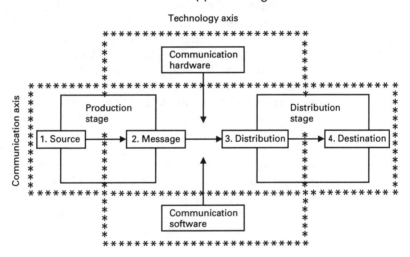

Fig. 9.2.1   Process of international communication (after Mowlana 1985).

The general aim of the model is to represent a familiar sequence from sender (1) to receiver (4), mediated by a technologically based production (2) and (3) a distribution system. In international communication, the situation differs from that at national level, in that each of the four stages can be (and often is) spatially, organizationally and culturally separated from the other stages. A source in one country (e.g., a politician or an advertiser) may be incorporated in a message produced in another country (e.g. a news bulletin) and distributed in that or even a third country. More commonly, the whole production stage is carried out in one country and distributed and received in another. This is how the richer 'north' is often related to the poorer 'south'. In less developed countries there will often be a considerable 'gap' (cultural, social, economic) between sources, message production and distribution system on the one hand and the world of the potential recipient on the other.

This typically extended and discontinuous process is cross-cut by the 'technology axis', which reminds us that each stage in the process is dependent on two kinds of expertise; relating to hardware or software. Production hardware consists, for instance, of studios and printing presses, distribution hardware of transmitters, satellite links, home receivers, etc. Production software includes such elements as scripts, performance rights, management and professional norms. Distribution software includes publicity, research and marketing. At both stages (production and distribution), Mowlana reminds us that there are 'extra-' as well as 'intra-' media variables – on the production side, facts of ownership and economics for instance and on the distribution side also social and economic factors which determine whether or not information actually flows through international channels.

Perhaps the most important point which the model illustrates and can help to analyse is the condition of multiple dependency which is often involved, especially in the flow of communication from more developed to less developed countries. The latter are often dependent in respect of all four main elements in the sequence and each may be controlled from the originating country.

Full communication autonomy can only be achieved when a country is self-sufficient in terms of both hardware and software and of both the means of production and of distribution. This self-sufficiency has to extend beyond the 'intra-media' elements to ownership and control and to the social context of supply and demand. Autonomy does not have to mean complete exclusion of international communication, but implies a potential for self-sufficiency which for most of the developing world is out of reach and even receding.

Reference   Mowlana, H. (1985) *International Flows of Information: A Global Report and Analysis*. Paris: Unesco.

9.3   INTERNATIONAL NEWS FLOW

Since the early 1950s, much evidence has accumulated from research on international news (e.g. Schramm 1964) to show that the flow of news is both very selective and one-directional. Organizational gatekeeping and the application of news values (Ch. 6) ensure that news is chosen to reflect the interests of the audiences of the large 'news-producing' countries. The dominance of the world news business by a few large agencies reinforces the bias in the content of what is available for many news media around the world. In one study of foreign news reporting, Galtung and Ruge (1965) showed how organizational and social-cultural factors led to a predominance of news in 'northern' news media which was implictly negative towards the Third World – tending to portray it as unstable, undemocratic and disaster-prone.

The situation fits the pattern described above in relation to the Mowlana model (Fig. 9.2.1). News sources, actual news stories, the means of international transmission and delivery to audiences are concentrated in the 'North'. For the media of dependent countries, there is no effective alternative to making use of the international news facilities which serve the developed world. While there are some benefits from the relatively low costs of the services, there are also drawbacks, especially arising from the unintended importation of the perspectives and values of the countries for whom the news supplies were originally produced. One of the costs has been referred to – the importation of a negative or pessimistic vision of their own region (e.g. Africa). If not negatively portrayed, Third World countries are simply often invisible on the stage of world events.

The situation has been explained in terms of a 'centre–periphery' model of news flow (Mowlana 1985, based on the work of Galtung) as shown in Fig. 9.3.1.

According to this model, the world is divided either into dominant central or dependent peripheral lands, with a predominant news flow from the former towards the latter. The larger, 'central' news-originating lands have their own 'satellites', although these

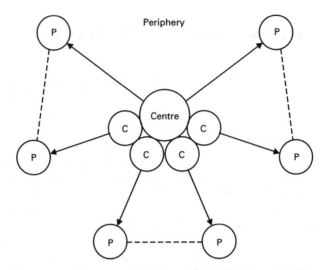

Periphery

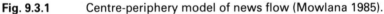

Fig. 9.3.1   Centre-periphery model of news flow (Mowlana 1985).

are much less dependent and have their own news-gathering and processing resources. Other hypotheses which the model represents are:

- that there will be a predominance of 'centre' news events reported in other media systems;
- 'centre' news is relatively more prominent in foreign news content of 'periphery' news media;
- there is little or no flow between peripheral countries themselves (absent or dotted line in model).

Quite a lot of support for these hypotheses has been found in research into news content. It is worth noting that the two formerly competing power blocs of East and West each constituted competing 'centres', although with their own relation of relative imbalance (more news flowed from West to East than vice versa). The model in Fig. 9.3.1 also fails to represent the extent to which there are *regional* (in the global sense) patterns of news flow and dependency, which does lead to some intra-peripheral news relationships. For instance, there are patterns which interrelate some Far-Eastern countries, the Caribbean, Latin American and North African sub-regions. This supports the view that there is no single centre and changes under way in world power and economics will continually modify the reality.

An additional feature of the situation is illustrated in Fig. 9.3.2 (also from Mowlana 1985), which shows how news is processed as between North and South.

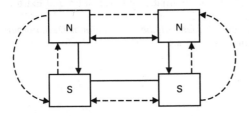

Fig. 9.3.2   North South 'round flow' model of news (Mowlana 1985).

The model shows strong vertical flows from North to South and also horizontal flows within the North. The return flows from South to North and within the South are weaker. The additional aspect of the case is provided by the fact that international news is often gathered in the South by correspondents from the North, where it returns to be processed and edited before its eventual return for distribution by the local media in the South. This process parallels the trade relations between the two 'blocs', such that raw materials flow north and return as expensive and not always appropriate manufactured goods. It also illustrates the proposition in the earlier model (Fig. 9.2.1) that autonomy requires control of software (news sources and processing facilities) as well as hardware (distribution facilities).

The pattern of flow of international news is strongly shaped by existing political and economic structures, but there are other contributory factors which can only be revealed by reference to what Rosengren (1970) has called 'extra-media' data. For instance, many researchers have shown that international news flows do not reflect either the realities of population size or geographic extent (e.g. Gerbner and Marvanyi 1977). It has been shown, however, that they do bear some relation to other objective factors, especially patterns of trade between nations and political relations (as shown by treaties and alliances). They also reflect cultural and language affinities and geographic proximity.

References   Galtung, J. and Ruge M. (1965) 'The structure of foreign news', *Journal of Peace Research*, **1**: 64–90.

Gerbner, G. and Marvanyi G. (1977) 'The many worlds of the world's press', *Journal of Communication*, **27 (1)**: 10–27.

Mowlana, H. (1985) *International Flows of Information: A Global Report and Analysis*. Paris: Unesco.

Rosengren, K.E. (1970) 'International news: Intra and Extra media data'. *Acta Sociologica*, **13**: 96–109.

Schramm, W. (1964) *Mass Media and National Development*. Stanford, CA: Stanford University Press.

9.4 TRANSNATIONAL TELEVISION FLOWS

Many of the basic patterns described also apply to the flow of media content other than news, especially to television fiction and entertainment. This type of content is often expensive to produce according to the standards of the global media industry. Many developed 'centre' countries are themselves relatively dependent in respect of audiovisual fiction. The dominance of the United States as world producer and supplier dates from the early period of the film industry (Tunstall 1977) and has been reinforced latterly, by the rapid growth of television. The flow of television programming has been charted in several studies (e.g. Varis 1974 and 1984), mainly by studying the composition of television schedules in receiving countries. Early research showed the degree to which nascent television systems of developing countries were dependent on foreign (mainly American) programme imports. The rapid advance of cable and satellite delivery and the relative decline of national public television monopolies has opened the way for an accelerating cultural 'invasion' of many European countries, especially by way of new commercial channels (De Bens and Kelly 1992). The scale and significance of these trends are still being debated, but the possibility of national and European cultural subordination and decline has been aired.

The evidence has been carefully assessed by Sepstrup (1989) and he has also suggested a model of the stages of 'transnationalization' of television. The debate tends to assume that international flow is an independent variable and that 'transnationalization' is a dependent variable or effect. In fact, as Sepstrup points out, there is no simple or direct cause and effect sequence at work, or not one that can be demonstrated. A distinction has first to be made between three kinds of international flow:

- **National**: where foreign (not home-produced) content is distributed in the national television system.
- **Bilateral**: where content originating in and intended for one country is received directly in a neighbouring country (e.g.

reception of British TV in Ireland or Dutch TV in Belgium).
- **Multilateral**: where content is produced or disseminated without a specific national audience in mind (as by some branches of the film industry or multinational satellite television services).

Each of these types of flow may have a different implication for effects and the balance between the three varies from place to place.

Sepstrup also underlines the sequence of *stages* by which any 'transnationalizing' effect has to be achieved:

1. Content has to be distributed (in any of the above three ways).
2. Content has to be received (often unpredictable and rarely proportional to the supply).
3. It has to have some *effect* (beyond reception) on how people think, what they know or how they behave, for 'transnationalization' of culture to be accomplished.

This can also be considered as a two-step process of effect in which 'transnationalized' TV services (those with much foreign content) are, first of all a *dependent* variable. This is a 'first level' effect. At the second step, transnationalized media are themselves an *independent* variable, with a potential for influencing society, values or culture, if the content is received and registered. Only if the second stage is completed is there a complete sequence of transnationalization. The main elements discussed are combined in a single model of TV transnationalization (Fig. 9.4.1) showing the relations between two countries (X and Y) in global environment of multilateral flow.

As portrayed, country X is a dominant supplier of television, although bilateral flows are not necessarily imbalanced. Both country X and Y are shown in the model as recipients of multilateral flows, although often the countries which tend to receive more bilateral flow are also greater recipients of multilateral supply. The model represents the case of television, but a rather similar pattern applies to popular music, a media industry dominated by a few large producing countries and firms and even more internationalized in distribution than is television.

There is another possible transnationalizing effect which is not shown in the model and that is the effect which occurs on home-

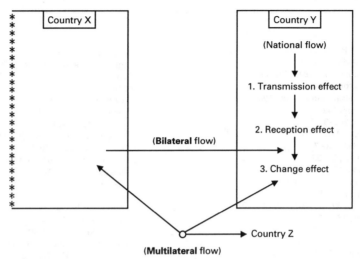

Fig. 9.4.1   Internationalization of television (based on theory on Sepstrup 1989).

produced content as a result of imitating or adapting foreign formats and genres. This is a significant *amplification* of the first level effect and much less easy to determine by normal methods of content research. As with news, there are a good many factors which play a part in the transnationalizing process, especially cultural and economic conditions. The degree of transnationalization (at first and second levels of effect) varies a good deal according to the specific type of content and from one country to another (depending on language and cultural affinities).

References   De Bens, E. and Kelly, M. (1992) 'TV content: Dallasification of culture?' pp. 75–100 in Siune, K. and Truetzschler, W. (eds.) *Dynamics of Media Politics*. London: Sage.

Sepstrup, P, (1989) 'Research into international television flows', *European Journal of Communication*, 4, 4: pp. 393–407.

Tunstall, J. (1977) *The Media are American*. London: Constable.

Varis, T. (1974) 'Global traffic in television', *Journal of Communication*, 24, 1: 102–9.

Varis, T. (1984) 'The international flow of TV progammes', *Journal of Communication*, 34, 1: 143–52.

INDEX